Early Praise for *Praying in God's Theater*

Joel Watts' *Praying in God's Theatre* brings a brilliant and fresh viewpoint to the *Book of Revelation*. For those of you laymen or women, like myself, who have struggled with the meaning and nature of Revelation, no matter how many bible studies, *Praying in God's Theatre* brings a spirited context to the Bible's most controversial and enigmatic book.

A few years ago I filmed a documentary on contemplative prayer, *Be Still*, with Beth Moore, Mac Lucado, Peter Kreeft, Dallas Willard, and Robert Foster; but that documentary pales in comparison with the soulful observation that Mr. Watts is able to imbue in this remarkable literary and academic work regarding the contemplation of *Revelation*.

Mr. Watts returns to the grand tradition of "Lectio Divina" in which scripture and reader become one. What did the Yale Humanities Professor, Harold Bloom say? "You don't read Shakespeare, Shakespeare reads you." What Mr. Watts is suggesting in his smart but easy-to-read book is that a prayerful spirited heart is truly necessary so that *Revelation can,* in a way, *read you.* In so doing, this process brings new levels of vision in one's own faith journey through the Holy Spirit.

In his remarkable book, Mr. Watts creates a practical pathway with a collection of wonderful prayers that will help the reader gain further insight into the mystic realms of the *Revelation* text. For so long, Fundamentalists have kidnapped the era in which we live. They have roped it around the end-of-days gloom seemingly inherent in *Revelation*. That interpretation only drives away the possibility of a truly meaningful life through Christ. Mr. Watts takes us to another place. "This is not just a chapter (*Revelation*) about endings, it is about new beginnings," he writes. In his thoughtful and powerful way, he allows us to unlock "the most important message" of the "Fifth Gospel."

What I admire about Watt's writing is that it is inclusive. It brings "the body of Christ" together. His intelligent and compassionate analysis hopefully strikes up a new kind of revival in which all brothers and sisters in Christ can partake. As a body, we have become so closed to discourse especially in the realms of science. Mr. Watts' view point on scripture, opens us up, frees us, allows us to engage with others in, healthy, life-affirming ways.

Praying in God's Theatre is for anyone who has struggled with *Revelation*. It opens your eyes and heart and mind to a fresh start. It may indeed alter your worldview in a way that will be surprising, loving, and Christ-like.

—David Paul Kirkpatrick

Author, and former President of Paramount Pictures, and Walt Disney Pictures

I found this book to be a very spiritually Christian book. The hand of God can be seen throughout the prayers

—Doug Iverson

Baptist, Ripon, Wisconsin

Joel L. Watts has incorporated a great blend of the teachings and liturgy from the Old Testament, its Psalms and ancient churches of the New Testament. His inclusion of the early church fathers, church councils and some of the greatest theologians throughout history Catholic, Orthodox and Protestant bridges it all together. This book is a great tool for understanding prayers, the liturgy, and the union of the Sacraments with Christ. It provides an in-depth perspective into Revelation and the Liturgy

—Most Reverend Kevin B. Twohig

East Coast Diocese of the Advent Independent Catholic Church

Joel L. Watts' innovative reading of the Book of Revelation continues his tradition of opening Scripture from a new and fresh perspective and offering readers a unique take on texts. Praying Scripture—even if that Scripture is the Apocalypse—is a spiritual exercise many of the Ancients endorsed. Joel's attempt to revive the practice is commendable.

—Jim West

Professor of Biblical Studies, Quartz Hill School of Theology

In this work on the book of Revelation, Joel L. Watts has did an excellent job of utilizing the best of contemporary exegesis as well as the words of the Church Mothers and Fathers. This will not doubt be an important resource for worship settings as local churches continue to embody the traditions of the early Church passed down to us.

—Rod Thomas

ThM (Master of Theology), and Baptist writer and political commentator at PoliticalJesus.com

With the entirety of the Christian tradition acting as his palate, Watts opens up one of the Bible's most mystifying and polarizing books. Rather than let John's Apocalypse sit in stasis, Watts uses the discipline of prayer to open it to those all over the Christian spectrum. This book is proof that—liberal or conservative—Revelation doesn't have to scare us.

—Rev. Chris Tiedeman

United Methodist Church (Indiana)

In this engaging and practical approach to the book of Revelation, Watts provides us with a wealth of information, sources, traditions, and even theologies that it is difficult to imagine how he was able to interweave them so seamlessly. In fact, for those that are interested in ecumenism, religious synthesis and even in syncretism, I cannot recommend this book enough as an example of how different Christian traditions can be joined together successfully for means of Christian devotion.

Personally, for a person that was brought up in a theology similar to the author's, this volume is such a breath of fresh air, and, accessible scholarship, that I cannot emphasize enough how helpful it has been to understand and enjoy the book of Revelation anew.

In a very fortuitous way, I was recently asked to write a course on the book of Revelation for a local parish church. You can be assured that this book will be in my required reading list.

—Daniel E. Ortiz MA MTh BTh

Ordained Pastor in the UCE (Bolivian Congregationalist Church) Denomination. (Presently an Anglican communicant and, soon to be, Doctoral candidate in Pentecostal and Charismatic Studies in The University of Birmingham, U.K.)

I once stood in the cave on the Island of Patmos where the ancient traditions of the church believed that the Apostle John received a revelation from God concerning the final triumph of the "Lamb that was slain." Centuries of scholarship have revised our understanding of the origins of the Book of Revelation, but its promises and images continue to fascinate the contemporary disciples of Jesus.

In this fascinating book, Joel Watts has transformed those promises and images into prayers, and has shifted the focus of our fascination with this book from our theology to our spirituality. As I moved through the pages of this book, I found nourishment for my spiritual life as I prayed the ancient vision of the triumphant and reigning Christ and I trust that it will be the same for each reader. This book is creative, profound, and spiritually provocative.

—William Boyd Grove

Bishop, Retired, United Methodist Church

Praying in God's Theater

Praying in God's Theater

Meditations on the Book of Revelation

JOEL L. WATTS

WIPF & STOCK · Eugene, Oregon

PRAYING IN GOD'S THEATER
Meditations on the Book of Revelation

Copyright © 2014 Joel L. Watts. All rights reserved. Except for brief quotations in critical publications or reviews, no part of this book may be reproduced in any manner without prior written permission from the publisher. Write: Permissions, Wipf and Stock Publishers, 199 W. 8th Ave., Suite 3, Eugene, OR 97401.

Wipf & Stock
An Imprint of Wipf and Stock Publishers
199 W. 8th Ave., Suite 3
Eugene, OR 97401

www.wipfandstock.com

ISBN 13: 978-1-62564-193-9

Manufactured in the U.S.A.

Quotes of Oecumenius' *Commentary on the Apocalypse* are taken from *Greek Commentaries on Revelation* translated by William C. Weinrich, edited by Thomas C. Oden. Copyright(c) 2011 by William C. Weinrich, Thomas C. Oden, Gerald L. Bray, Michael Glerup and the Institute for Classical Christian Studies. Used by permission of InterVarsity Press, PO Box 1400, Downers Grove, IL 60515. www.ivpress.com

Scripture quotations taken from the Revised English Bible, copyright © Oxford University Press and Cambridge University Press 1989. All rights reserved.

To those who taught me to pray
and to my children who cause me to pray

More things are wrought by prayer than this world dreams of.
Wherefore, let thy voice rise like a fountain for me night and day.

Alfred, Lord Tenneyson ("Morte D'Arthur")

Contents

Introduction   1

1. The Introit   9
2. The Penitential Prayer   21
3. The Beatific Vision   40
4. The Presentation of the Gospel, Part I   50
5. The Presentation of the Gospel, Part II   63
6. The Triumphal Hymn   75
7. The Prayers of the Faithful   84
8. The Preparation for the Great Entrance   94
9. The Cherubic Hymn   105
10. The Great Entrance   112
11. The Presentation of Israel, the Church, and Mary   124
12. The Presentation of the Church Triumphant   135
13. The Presentation of Jesus   145
14. The Heavenly Choir   157
15. To End God's Wrath   162
16. Prayers of Confession   177
17. The Table of the Lord   185
18. A Homily—The Eucharistic Vision   197
19. The Prayer of Dismissal   210

Afterword by Major Jeff Carter, Salvation Army   219

Bibliography   223

Introduction

> "Prayer is the elevation of the heart,
> not the breath or voice alone."[1]

P rayer is a constant refrain in the Christian experience. The role prayer performs in our faith is expressed best by the phrase *Lex orandi, lex credenda*.[2] In the earliest pages of the Scriptures we read of direct interactions between God and his creation, communing with us as a reminder we are not a solitary instance in the cosmos. The Psalms are Israel's testimony in prayer. The Prophets and the Psalmists are not alone in drawing us to prayer; we find Jesus enforcing this wisdom when he imparts the *Our Father*. Paul was known to quote hymns of the early communities as he engaged his audience. The writers of the early Church, Mystics, and the Reformers all sought to impart the need for a heart elevated through prayer. Throughout the most difficult days, when we are rent asunder by

---

1. "Commentary on True and False Religion," section 25 on "Prayer" (Z III, 851ff) as quoted by Jim West in *Christ Our Captain*, 22. See West's chapter on Zwingli and Prayer.

2. From the Latin, meaning, "the law of prayer is the law of belief." It is the concept that our worship is based on belief, preceding the canons and creeds of Christianity. "Let us consider the sacraments of priestly prayers, which having been handed down by the Apostles are celebrated uniformly throughout the whole world and in every Catholic Church so that the law of praying might establish the law of believing." (St. Proper of Aquitaine, in Migne, *Patrologia Latina* 51:209–10).

the forces of this world, we turn to prayer for comfort and to speak directly to our God.

In oppression's labors prayer is born, from prayer springs hope, from hope comes resistance. Resistance gives way to liberation.

Christians, whether we know it or not, are blessed with a beautiful tradition of mystics who have turned prayer from the external to the internal and thus set the world on fire. I do not intend to do that, nor should you. However, if we turn the prayer from asking God to do our bidding to elevating our spirit to the Divine we may in fact spark something that does grow into a great revival. Or, we might just find it easier to get through a terrible season of our lives.

John once wrote a book intending to reveal to his readers a message from Jesus of a hopeful resistance. For many it is the only book in the canon, while others are surprised such a book exists! Some use it to read the newspaper while a few ignore it except when necessary, when the Lectionary inserts it into a reading or perhaps at a funeral (Revelation 21:5). Many books are sold trying to interpret it only to expose the sad reality that John's most important message is still hidden.

Perhaps our modern eyes have simply lost focus. Are we so arrogant today to believe John's original message was lost so soon after it was delivered?

Ian Boxall writes, "there are good grounds for proposing that the book was designed for reading during Christian gatherings for worship, probably the Eucharist."[3] He calls this the "threatre of reception." You will find a singular theme in much of the commentary below. I believe the Eucharist is always in view.[4] With each reading of certain key words and acknowledging certain tropes my conviction grew. I began to see Revelation as the key to understanding the

---

3. Boxall, *The Revelation of Saint John*, 15.

4. St. Irenaeus, (*Against Heresies*, 4.18.5) stated his belief on the Eucharist, an important element to this present work. "Our opinion is in accordance with the Eucharist, and the Eucharist in turn establishes our opinion." This is in the same mold as St. Proper of Aquitaine. See above.

earliest reception of the Eucharist as well as the origin of ancient liturgies. John's message was not lost but kept safe in the ancient liturgies of the Church Universal. These ancient liturgies, as I propose and I hope you see, were built upon John's Apocalypse. These celebrations grew from a source—*lex orandi, lex credenda.*

This is not to say the author of Revelation did not hide in his poem an attack on the enemies of the Church. Instead, like the dough of the Eucharist wherein the priest works in yeast, flour, and olive oil, John begins to work into the ancient liturgical celebration elements of his context. The author is a Jewish believer in Jesus as the Messiah who has survived the Jewish Revolt with his faith intact. Beginning with the sacrament given by Jesus, the Eucharist, John begins to sing a song celebrating the triumph of the Church over Rome. We are undefeatable when we unite with Jesus through the proper administration of the body and the blood. Jesus is always present even in our oppression if we celebrate the Eucharist. Thus, the book has become something more than prayers. Instead it is a way to pray with John anew, but it is likewise a call to communion with one another in Jesus.

The impetus of this project is manifold. I grew up believing Jesus would soon return only to bring wrath and destruction to all. This sparked an interest in my own studies as I tried to determine the *real* meaning of Revelation. My initial inclination was like the great majority of Christianity, to see it as a book yet unfulfilled. After studying the book for years, I gave up. All of the inroads I made or would make, or may make, into Revelation I have discovered to be somewhat inadequate. Revelation is not about what will happen (futurist) or even what happened (historicist), but what is always happening above us. It is quite simply, a book envisioning Christ enthroned through suffering, something the Eucharist represents.

My upbringing fueled my present motivation. Living for so long with Revelation as something far distant, I sought to bring it closer. In a seminary class on worship, I was tasked with a final project. This allowed me to bring my interest to life in this regard. I believe

Scripture is never far from us and yet we put it behind a Christian patina, shrouded with theology and doctrine. Scripture is theology; however, it is a theology in motion rather than theology at rest.

For my project, because it is filled with scenes of worship and praise I sought to treat Revelation as a liturgical book. I felt Revelation could serve as a basis of prayers for liturgical churches much like Isaac Watts who first turned the Psalms into English hymnody. As I brought the project to a conclusion, I found a certain mystical solace in individuals praying through Revelation in such a way as to hear it rather than read it. By examining closely the movement of Revelation while fine-tuning the praying drama of liturgy, something between John and I happened. Revelation became something else.

Recently I was introduced to Christian mysticism but understood only a small fraction what these saints were trying to do with their prayers and life lead in service to Christ. They were seeking a union like no other. In writing these prayers and saying them, sometimes aloud or sometimes whispers in hushed tones within my mind's megaphone, I grew closer to God in Christ, seeing more and more the promise of the Fifth Gospel in John's work. Hearing John speak of the cosmic Christ, a door was opening before me and I walked in.

What I did not know then, but now have a better understanding, is how the mystics and the ancient liturgists shared the theme of a union with Christ through the Eucharist. Their prayers are not simple requests or longwinded speeches pleading for God's mercy. Their daily actions were meant to purify their souls so as to meet God in the open door.

While I hope the prayers in this book will be used for liturgical prayers shared between congregation and leader or between two friends at lunch time (or when you are alone with God, let John speak his part and you rejoin) performed on the grand stage before God, my primary goal is to open to others what has been opened or me. It is my hope that by praying the prayers and meditating upon the words herein, most of them not mine, that a closer union with Christ can be had.

Theology of This Book

I am a United Methodist Christian; however, my tendencies lie with the deeper spirituality found in the Roman Catholic Church. Some will find this book awash with Catholic theology while others will see Protestantism, albeit a Wesleyan version, guiding the interpretation of such theology. It may be better imagined the author has one foot in the Tiber and one in the Thames while breathing deeply the air from the East. If we are unable to learn from all of Christian history, then we will simply have no future. Thus, I will reach into all of Christian Tradition to reason out our Scriptural experience.

I take a rather high view of the sacraments, specifically the Eucharist. Likewise, I believe our deeds play a part in our final reward. This is a not a book meant to undergird either of those two suspicions; this is simply a book wherein I occasionally make use of those personal fundamentals.

In regards to the concepts of contemplative unity and certain unity discussed throughout this book, I draw these concepts from St. John of the Cross, a Carmelite monk. In *The Dark Night of the Soul*, St. John argues that our progression as Christians begin in the Obscure Night, but as we move along by meditation and prayer, we will pass through various stages until we reach the Contemplative State, or the divine union with God. We do this through purgative contemplation. I would differ slightly with the ancient monk here, arguing instead our contemplative state is that state in which we seek unity with God through purgative contemplation but is never fully achieved until we have the fully realized union. Rather, we are reaching *for* the ideal while we pray. Scripturally speaking, it is working out our own salvation. The certain unity is that offered in the Eucharist. Baptism sets us in union with Christ, but it is the celebration of the Eucharist causing the full unity with the divine.

The picture I attempt to paint with Revelation's brush is an attempt to achieve both unities. Our prayers will incorporate many mysteries on the way to the certain unity that is the Eucharistic

Celebration of the sacrifice of Christ. Contemplative unity places us in the process of purging ourselves of those things unbecoming of accepting the Son of God into ourselves. We attempt to reach the ideal state by going on to perfection (a concept highlighted among Protestants by John Wesley) through the deeds of prayers while knowing nothing will bring us as close to the divine as the Eucharist in this life and the call to arise into the life eternal. Finally, contemplative unity is the "already, but not yet" event in our Christian journey.

In regards to the notion of what many call contemplative prayer, I do not see it as an otherworldly experience meant to engender something of an inspired message, prophecy, or personal revelation. Rather, as St. John of the Cross says, it is "the purgation of sense" and "is merely the gate and entrance of contemplation, and serves rather to harmonize sense and spirit than to unite the latter with God. The stains of the old man still remain in the mind, though not visible, and if they be not removed by the strong soap and lye of the purgation of this night, the mind cannot attain to the pureness of the Divine union."[5] The contemplative unity we seek is this purgation of the self. Prayer should elevate us away from ourselves and not seek anything else but a preparation for God.

My position on the crucial impetus of this book is this: John wrote after the destruction of the Jewish Temple, a momentous event in Judaism. Identities were created in this moment, eventually spawning rabbinical Judaism and what came to be known as Christianity. The outcome of this event, however, became enshrined in the developing Mishnah and the liturgies developing in the Christian sect. The rabbis preserved the practices of the Temple in Jewish literature while building a theological argument for Temple-less Judaism. John does the same thing, albeit with Jesus as the center.

He takes pre-existing liturgical language of the Jesus followers to construct a liturgical story with a theological argument, although we should not think they are completely separate, of the Church as the *new* Temple. Again we repeat *lex orandi, lex credenda*. John reveals

5. Saint John of the Cross, *The Dark Night of the Soul*, 375.

how Jesus wins the victory over the Romans and the enemies of the community by examining (his) world events from the viewpoint of heaven. Just as the Gospels reveal Jesus on earth, John reveals Jesus in heaven.

How to Use This Book

The second verse of the first Psalm speaks to the delight one finds meditating day and night upon the words of God. Stories abound throughout Scripture of God's people doing the same thing. When Ezra led the Jews out of the Exile, he realized he must instruct God's people in the Law of Moses. For weeks Ezra interpreted and meditated upon the words of Moses until a revival occurred (Nehemiah 8:1—9:38). The Church became the only thing holding European civilization together after the fall of the Roman Empire. Monasteries were built to once again call people back to a meditative life. Orders such as the Benedictines sprang up to lead their followers into praying Scripture, building their theology on the *lectio divino*. After the Protestant Reformation erupted, English hymn writers began to transform the Psalms into something resembling a Church hymn. Taking portions of Scripture to transform into prayers is not new but is a valid part of our Church heritage. I hope this book stands in that valuable Tradition.

Like call and response prayers, you will find portions in bold.[6] The bold sections of Scripture are based on (usually) Revelation, while the words in regular print are the literary sources for John's writing. John used a tremendous amount of Scriptural allusions drawn from the New Testament and other works while drafting his work. I will make use of many of them to provide an answer to him. I have tried to arrange it so John's words are met with similar words or thoughts from other writers of the faith. For individuals, you should alternate praying aloud either the bold or the regular while mediating upon

---

6. I am not the Psalmist; these prayers are not perfect. They are mine. I would encourage you to draft your own, on how you would like to pray Scripture.

the opposite of your first choice. For two or more participants, let one take the bold and the other the regular. For congregations, you may take portions of these prayers and use them at will.

Surrounding the prayers are mediations and devotions from saints throughout the ages. You will find familiar names like John Wesley and maybe a few unfamiliar ones like St. Bonaventure and a sixth century theologian by the name of Oecumenius. This is an ecumenical book, so you will hear Catholic and Orthodox voices as well as Protestant ones. You will also experience some jolting meditations, such as praying for our enemies and contemplating an intermediate state.

The best way to use this book is as a spiritual discipline. Every chapter of Revelation is represented in his book, but many of them are split into several prayers. I would encourage you to break them up however you see fit. I have set a pattern that appeals to me, but if you find one that suites you, use it. For instance, I have split the first chapter of Revelation between two prayers. Maybe you want three, four, or five (to mirror the daily offices). That is fine. But, maintain these prayers and devotionals. Let Scripture live in such a way that is active to you and in you.

1

The Introit

"Three times in the day you should pray."[1]

Our prayers in this chapter serve as a prologue to the entire book. Regardless of John's reason, either the Roman Empire or something more distressing, inspired Scripture provides for us a continued application. In the Epistle to the Hebrews, the author tells us several times the Holy Spirit is speaking through the ancient text. Therefore, regardless of John's writing, we can still hear the Spirit of God speaking through the text today, to us in such a way as to reinvigorate this book.

We hear the connections to other books of the canon, including the Psalms, Ecclesiastes, Daniel and Zechariah as well as Romans. These books were a part of the author's library, serving to sustain him in his time of need as well as to bolster the confidence of the suffering audience.

I use the familiar term sustain here. Scripture is John's repast. He feasts on Scripture. It becomes to him a sacrament, communicating grace to him in his time of need. Origen, a third century theologian, writes "His flesh and blood . . . are the divine Scriptures, eating

---

1. Didache 8.3.

Praying in God's Theater

which, we have Christ; the words becoming his bones, the flesh becoming the meaning from the texts, following which meaning, as it were, we see in a mirror dimly the things which are to come."[2] It is not a coincidence John later eats the words of the book (Revelation 10:10), for they themselves become to him the same sacrament he has found in ancient writings.

What drove John to write? We really do not know. Revelation may have several levels of meaning to it. If it is purely a historical, albeit poetic, account of the Jewish War, we are left with the amazement as to why it was canonized. As I discussed above, John is writing a liturgical drama. He has turned to the worship of God during whatever situation he was experiencing. In doing so, he draws from his distinctly Jewish-Christian liturgy to produce a poem in the classical sense dedicated to proclaiming Jesus as King according to Psalm 2, professing a Eucharistic adoration, and in securing to his readers the proper mind for seeking the peace of God.

First Prayer: Revelation 1:1–6

We see the oppression across the world.
We see the tears of the oppressed
We see no comforter.
The oppressors are powerful, but their victims helpless.[3]
Where is the King of Glory?[4]

---

2. Origen, *Treatise on the Passover and Dialogue with Heraclides*, 4.

3. Ecclesiastes 4:1. I have chosen to use this verse to start the prayer because we often tend to overlook times when there was truly no hope for even God's people, or at least no hope in view. In a sermon once preached, I began with this verse only to turn to John 14–16. The comfort the author Ecclesiastes is looking for would not come until Jesus, through the Father, bestowed the Spirit. In Revelation, John is going to paint a severely hopeless picture in chapter 5 where God is in desperate need of someone qualified to open the book of life. In the distance, beyond the horizon of hope stands Jesus.

4. Psalm 24:7–10. In Paul's first letter to the Corinthians he calls Jesus the Lord of Glory (2:8). Here, I have used it to focus the entire structure of this book on identifying the central message of Revelation, that Jesus is the Lord of Glory.

The Introit

Let us hear the revelation from Jesus Christ,
Show us what is taking place.
Send us your angel to present to your faithful servant
This is the word of God.
Let us hear the testimony of Jesus Christ.

When in Egypt your people groaned as slaves and cried for help,
You, oh God, are who heard their groaning.
You remembered your covenant to Abraham, Isaac, and Jacob
And looked down on the people of Israel to act.

Bless us, oh God, as we hear the words of this prophecy
Bless all who listen and obey its message.
Together with Christ we are heirs of God's glory.
If we are to share his glory, let us also share his suffering.
Let us suffer this now for the glory to be revealed is too great to know.

Grace and peace to you

Grace and peace to you from the one who is,
The one who always was,
The one who is still to come.
We see the seven spirits before his throne and from Jesus Christ.
He is our faithful witness to these things,
He is the first to rise from the dead,
He is the ruler of all the kings of the world.

God has made him firstborn
He is higher than kings of the earth.
The heavens bear a faithful witness.
All glory to him who freed us from our sins by shedding his blood.

Wait just a little longer, O Creation
Wait for that day God will reveal us as children

Throughout the remainder of this book, when I use a verse from another part of the canon in the prayers, I will footnote them, often without commentary.

Creation joins us in our curse
But we are hopeful
We hope for the day when we are freed from death
All creation longs for this

He has made us a Kingdom of priests
Hear creation groaning as in the pains of childbirth even now.
We groan with it as believers who through the Holy Spirit have foretasted glory
We long for our bodies to be released from sin and suffering.

We wait with hope
God will give us the rights of heirs
We will be given new bodies by his promise.

He has made us a Kingdom of priests for God his Father.
All glory and power to him forever and ever!

Amen

Introit

In liturgical celebrations, the *introit* is the beginning of the service used to signify "the entrance of the Lord into the world in the Incarnation."[5] One Anglican theologian saw the entirety of the liturgical service from the Introit to the Offertory as a dramatic representation of the traditional Christian view of the Old Testament as a foreshadowing of Christ.[6] C.E. Hammond comments, "In reference to the Eucharistic Liturgies however it has either a general meaning equivalent to 'anthem,' or a special meaning applying to the Introit. A notion of alternate singing, or of repetition, is involved in the word. The Roman Introit consists of a verse (often called specially 'the Introit'), followed by a verse of a Psalm and the *Gloria Patri*, after which the first verse is repeated."[7] If we examine Revelation 1, we see an antiphonal resounding between Jesus and John acting as this introit.

---

5. Stone, *The Eucharistic Sacrifice*, 27.
6. Stone, *A History of the Doctrine of the Holy Eucharist*, 267.
7. Hammond, *Liturgies: Eastern and Western*, 376.

We begin our mystical descent into praying Revelation here as we would a liturgical celebration.

In the first prayer, we encounter words from John (Revelation 1:1–6) acting as the entry into the audience's mind, establishing himself and his message. Everything John says and does throughout this book is to serve one eventual purpose, to direct the believer to Jesus Christ who is the ontological victor. In this section, you will encounter words from the Psalmist and Paul, both who wrote of the love of God to us. This is Revelation's significance, to show the love of God as a path forward and to let us know we are God's ultimate concern.

All of Christian doctrine and theology can be traced to the Creation. The great circle of Christian Scripture begins with God creating in Genesis and ends with the complete renewal of that Creation in Revelation. Before God is Judge, before God is Savior, God is Creator. Adam was given dominion over the world, but fell, losing his kingdom to the powers of the air. In Revelation 1 Jesus steps from the clouds to begin to tell John a new earth is coming, when the zenith of God's creation will once again achieve that which we were meant to be—kings and priests.

The venerable Bede sees this book as something to drive the existent Church towards perfection.[8] Apringius of Beja in his work calls this perfection "obedience."[9] Do not simply hear what John has to say, but hear so intensely the sound of your heart becomes the ringing of the Gospel. This book becomes something much more than a path to the end of the age, but if we follow the Tradition of interpreters before us Revelation is revealed as a path to the glory of the Father and the Son.

Bede notes the uniqueness of the relationship between the Father and the Son, especially in these first few verses. This is not the Son's Glory, nor the Son's direct action, but it is the Father's through the Son's, echoing the writers of the New Testament (Colossians 1:13–20). We are able to see something of a glimpse of the genius of

8. Bede, *Explanation of the Apocalypse*, 1.1.
9. Apringius of Beja, *Tractate on the Apocalypse*, 1.3.

Christian doctors in these verses. The seeds of the Trinity are firmly planted by John so as to cause later commentators to pause here and reflect on this address.

Numbers are part of the mystery drawing us to Revelation. Seven is the number of the churches, spirits, lampstands, and angels. Andrew of Caesarea sees in seven the meaning of perfection.[10] Regardless of time and place, we are commanded to listen to John. John before and after the Nicene Councils of the fourth century declares that to everywhere the Three-in-One speaks. Like seven, the number three indicating God's completeness and unity are displayed. The Father is who was (or, transcendent), Jesus is who is (or, immanent), and the Spirit is who is to come (or, indwelling).

There is something here about Jesus as the firstborn of the dead. Jesus is not just our Lord and Savior, but also the exemplar, our pledge and our proof. In the second rejoinder, I used Exodus 2:23–24 for several reasons. First, Revelation is a mirror to Exodus as God's answer to the groaning of his people. Second, it calls to mind the Passover when the blood upon the door was used as a sign and pledge in God's relationship to Israel. As a sign it represented to the angel of death that the inhabitants of the house were God's people. As a pledge, God used it to represent the continuing sacrifice that would avert sin for a little while. Here, Jesus becomes our eternal Passover pledge. He has witnessed that God is faithful and as firstborn from the dead, God has given him as a pledge not just of the bodily resurrection, but likewise a guarantee God will never leave us in the hands of our enemies.

John calls his book a "revelation" (1:1) and a "prophecy" (1:3). What do these words mean? We are given daily doses of the wrong approach to the latter word. A prophecy is a not a prediction of what is to come far in the future. Not once in the Gospel do we find the word *prophēteia* (prophecy) applied to words of the Hebrew Prophets and used to validate the message of Jesus. The early followers of Christ understood the overall sayings of the Prophets in a much

---

10. Andrew of Caesarea, *Commentary on the Apocalypse,* 1.4.

The Introit

different way. If prophecy was acknowledged, it was generally in accordance with the notion of bringing something to a completion, or fulfillment (cf. Matthew 15:7). Additionally, Christ was encouraged from time to time to give a prophecy of the immediate surroundings. For the writers of the New Testament, prophecy is not foretelling, but unveiling.[11]

Philo, a first century Jewish exegete and philosopher said, "But since there is an infinite variety of both human and divine circumstances which are unknown both to king, and lawgiver, and chief priest, for a man is no less a created and mortal being from having all these offices, or because he is clothed with such a vast and boundless inheritance of honor and happiness, he was also of necessity invested with the gift of prophecy, in order that he might through the providence of God learn all those things which he was unable to comprehend by his own reason; for what the mind is unable to attain to, that prophecy masters."[12]

Paul tells us a prophet is for the encouragement of the Church (1 Corinthians 14:3). He or she is one who reveals (Revelation 1:1) what God is trying to communicate.[13] What is John's goal here? Is it *really* about some future event even he could not foresee? No. It is about God's message to the Church—and we much contend that it is for the Church Universal, including time and place—about the struggles between Heaven and Earth.

While reading and praying through John's communication, do not read so fast as to miss the nation of Israel. Throughout all of Revelation, it is difficult to distinguish the Church from Israel. It is made clear in John's language Israel is still in view with God's plan. "The lack of close New Testament verbal parallels to John's characterization of

11. I have written on this topic before, with some of this paragraph coming from a previous posting. See Unsettled Christianity, *Incarnational Fulfillment of the Prophets—A Conversation*, Accessed 5 August, 2013, http://unsettledchristianity.com/2010/05/incarnational-fulfillment-of-the-prophets-a-conversation/.

12. *The Life of Moses* 2:6, as translated by C.D. Yonge in *The Works of Philo Judaeus*, Volume 3, 1855.

13. See Deuteronomy 18:18, cf., Exodus 7:1–2.

Jesus in the doxology throws into sharp relief the presence of such parallels in the Old Testament . . . *The failure to understand what John is doing in the doxology leads many interpreters into much confusion regarding what they mistakenly view to be the separate roles of Israel and the Church in the visions that unfold.*"[14] There is a moment in ancient church history when Jews and Gentile Christians parted ways. While there is the drifting away, even into the fourth and fifth centuries, Jews and Christians were able to in many instances celebrate God together. Here, John is speaking directly to a Jewish-Christian audience. That should not alarm us today, as the path to Christianity begins with Judaism. We have to worship the singular God of the universe and understand we are placed into covenant with him by his grace along with Israel.

Second Prayer: Revelation 1.7–20

See him coming with the clouds.

Our eyes shall see him coming.

The eyes of those who pierced him will see him coming.
The Nations of the world will see him coming and they will mourn.

We see someone like a son of man coming with the clouds of heaven
He will pour out the spirit of grace and prayer on David,
On Jerusalem and on us.
We will look on him whom we have pierced
We will mourn for him as for our only child.

He is the Alpha and the Omega
He is the beginning and the end.
He is, he always was, and he is still to come
He is the Almighty One.

He is the Lord God

He is the First and the Last

14. Trafton, *Reading Revelation*, 20–21.

There is no other God besides him

He is the Lord, the Redeemer and King of Israel,
He is the Lord of Heaven's Armies.

John, our brother suffers with us in God's Kingdom
We must patiently endure as Jesus calls us.
He was exiled to the island of Patmos for preaching the word of God
Let us hear his testimony about Jesus.

He like us worshiped on the Lord's Day,
He was caught up in the Spirit of God.
A loud voice like a trumpet blast says,
"Write in a book everything you see,
"Send it to the seven churches of every time and place."

John is commanded to write in perfection to the Church in every time and place
So hear what the Spirit says to the Church.

Speak to us so that we may hear and be comforted
Let us hear and be obedient.

See the seven gold lampstands and see Jesus standing in the middle of the lampstands.
Hear him and see him wearing a long robe with a gold sash.
His head and his hair are white like wool,
His eyes are like flames of fire.
His feet are like polished bronze refined in a furnace.
Listen to his voice as it thunders like mighty ocean waves.
He holds seven stars in his right hand,
A sharp two-edged sword comes from his mouth.
His face is like the sun in all its brilliance.

We see one like a son of man coming with the clouds
We hear the voice, the flashes, and the voice of the Trumpet.
We are fearful and stand at a distance.
We see him and we fall at his feet, our bodies seized near death.
He lays his right hand on us and says,
"Don't be afraid!

"I am the First and the Last."

"Listen to me, O family of Jacob, Israel my chosen one!"

He alone is God

"I am the First and the Last, the living one, the one who died, but see me—
"I am alive forever and ever! And I hold the keys of death and the grave."

**We live, for we died and we are buried with Christ by baptism.
Just as Christ was raised from the dead by the Father's power, now too we have new lives. Because we are united with him in his death, We will also be raised to life as he is.**

Speak aloud what John saw
Tell of the tension of here and now and not yet.

**We know the meaning of the mystery of the seven stars
John saw in the Lord's right hand and the seven gold lampstands
The seven stars are the angels of the seven churches
The seven lampstands are the seven churches.**

Amen

The Little Entrance

"*The Little Entrance*, an oriental rite, is the solemn procession when the Book of the Gospels is brought from the *Prothesis* to the Holy Table."[15] We are not mistaken in seeing John as beginning his refrain with a quotation from the books of Zechariah and Daniel as if he is bringing Scripture into the sanctuary.

Zechariah 12:10, specifically, has found a distinctly awful use by Christians in their relationship with Jews; however, in normative Christian theology and practice, we should see ourselves in the

---

15. Hammond, *Liturgies: Eastern and Western*, 379. It is also called "Liturgy of the Gospel book." See Cross and Livingstone, *The Oxford Dictionary of the Christian Church*, 991.

words of both Zechariah and John. If Christ died for all of us before we sinned, then we were there when the Jewish leaders handed Jesus over to the Romans who pierced him. We know we are meant to see it this way because John alters the prophet's words to include a "whole earth" view. We are bound together, each and every one of us, in piercing Jesus and in seeing Jesus's return. What John is doing is to bring forth the Scriptures he has and place them before us to communicate grace.

The alert listener will already hear John's use of the Old Testament, with allusions given in such a way as to present John's work as the crowning achievement. As the prayers for the rest of this book are said, focus on the role Revelation has played in the canon. It mirrors Genesis, complete with bloody falls, snakes, and mysterious voices from heaven, acting as natural capstone for the Christian literary vault. Likewise, it acts as the wellspring of Christian doctrinal tradition.

Who is it that is the Alpha and Omega? John's language is purposely ambiguous here. In John's Gospel, we read Jesus is the agent through which God created the world. Tertullian reminds us he is the beginning and the end as portrayed in the Gospels and of every dispensation.[16] Since the godhead is indivisible where we see Jesus we see the Father.[17] As we move through the rest of the prologue, the person in view here becomes more clearly seen as Jesus. This is mirrored throughout the rest of John's book. Christ progresses from standing around the throne to sharing the throne with God the Father. When we pray we can be assured that our prayers are made to the indivisible Godhead, of the Father and the Son, the Alpha and the Omega.

As we close the chapter on this prayer, we need to ask ourselves the question that caused early Christians to write their creeds: Who is Jesus Christ? We can listen to well-meaning scholars who argue over the Historical Jesus and leave it there. Or, maybe we can listen

---

16. Tertullian, *On Monogamy*, 5.
17. St. Athanasius, *Discourses Against the Arian*, 3.4.

in on John's conservation here, and see Jesus as someone ahistorical. Is Jesus only set in history or does he control history? If Jesus is God, what is our proper response to him as God?

The Prayer of Adoration

> O God, you have revealed to us yourself
> By John, the Apostles, and the Prophets,
> By your Son, Jesus Christ, your Word
> Reveal to us now heaven's ordering
>
> O My Jesus, your servant John testified to you
> Let us now bear witness to what he saw
> Bless us as we read and pray what you have revealed us
> For your time is always near
>
> O Spirit of the Living God,
> Grant us Grace and Peace from the Lord
> He is; He was; He is to come forevermore
> Grant us peace from the seven spirits around the throne
>
> Oh My Jesus, you are the Father's faithful witness
> You are the firstborn of the dead, raised by the Spirit
> You are the king of kings
> It is by your previous blood we are released from our sins
> By you, we have become a kingdom of priests to God the Father
> Glory and Power be to him forever
>
> Lord, when we see in you the clouds
> We who have pierced you,
> We from all the tribes of the earth
> We will mourn for our sins
> Amen; Amen.
>
> O Lord God, you are the Alpha and the Omega
> You are the one who is, who was, and who will come
> You alone are Almighty

2

The Penitential Prayer

> "Fear not to appear little and contemptible, or to be called by men fools and madmen; but announce penance in simplicity, trusting in Him who overcame the world by humility."[1]

The role of penance is often chided in Protestant circles, but it is a longstanding tradition with an aim at moving the penitent to prayerfully consider his or her sins before God.[2] St. John of the Cross, in writing of Jacob in Genesis 35, notes the continuous removal of sin. "He must cast away the strange gods, the earthly affections and attachments. He must purify himself from the impressions which the desires have made on the soul, in the obscure night of sense, denying them and doing penance duly for them, and, in the third place,

---

1. St. Francis of Assisi, as found in Butler, *The Lives of the Fathers, Martyrs and Other Principal Saints, Vol. 4*, 47.
2. Penance is a sorely misunderstood term. Perhaps the best, and easily accessible understanding of it is found in Peter Jackson's recent film adaptation of J. R. R. Tolkien's *The Hobbit*. In one scene, the gray wizard addresses his love of the fictional hobbits. He says, "Saruman believes it is only great power that can hold evil in check, but that is not what I have found. I found it is the small everyday deeds of ordinary folk that keep the darkness at bay . . . small acts of kindness and love."

he must change his garments."³ In other words, it is not simply an outside act that removes our sins, but what some call a "*sacramental exchange*."⁴ This is not about the initial act of grace, but the continued procession to perfection.⁵

The following prayers are centered on the penitent who, sorrowful for their sins, stands in purgative contemplation. I have constructed the prayers to place the precant as the Church in question. If Revelation is written to the Church Universal, we can identify times in the life of the Church befitting each of the Asian churches. Below, I will make the argument we must participate in Revelation as the condemned. For now, however, we can identify those times in our own lives where we have succumbed to moments of doubt or even apostasy. Yet, God is just and faithful to forgive our sins if we confess them (1 John 1:9).

There are seven churches and thus seven prayers. As I have said, seven is likely to be a sign that the end audience of John's work is the Church Universal; however, there is another possibility. "A hint of higher things is seen in the belief that the ultimate happiness of the just lies in communion with God. Some Rabbis distinguished seven degrees of the just (accommodated to the seven heavens); only the seventh and highest degree 'sees God.' This conception is not that of the beatific vision in Christian theology."⁶ Once we pass through

---

3. Saint John of the Cross, *The Ascent of Mount Carmel*, 25.

4. Armstrong, *Biblical Catholic Answers for John Calvin*, 166.

5. Wesley struggled with Roman Catholic doctrines of penance, as he did with other "popish" doctrines; however, this does not mean he disagreed completely. "The view of auricular confession, which, as has been said, John Wesley held at Oxford, was not entirely discarded by him in later life, but underwent a curious change. It may possibly be yet another proof of Wesley's devotion to primitive practice that he should have sought to get behind private confession, and to reintroduce a system which certainly bore some points of resemblance to that which was known in the Early Church as 'public penance.'" Taylor, *John Wesley and the Anglo-Catholic Revival*, §3. See also Wesley's sermons 40 and 76.

6. McKenzie, *The Jewish World in New Testament Times*, 740. See also Josephus's discussion on the spatial aspects of the Temple in *War* 1.26 and *Apion* 2.102–4. Like wise, St. Thomas Aquinas sees seven degrees of humility in

these seven churches, or the seven mansions of St. John of the Cross, we will indeed see God.

The First Prayer: Revelation 2:1–7

Lord, let us confess our sins to you,
We are like the Church of Ephesus
We work patiently and suffer many things
But we do not tolerate the wicked
We test the spirits and those who claim to be apostles
We have found so many false teachers
Let us never grow weary in the cause of the Gospel

O Lord, we know your promise to remove your angel from us
We have lost our first love,
We have lost the love you have given us
We are too high and we must repent
Favor us, O Lord, and give to your people freedom

O God, speak to us with the Spirit
Let us heed your promise to be victorious
Give to us the right to eat from the tree of life standing in the Garden of God

Amen

Anselm, writing that he "gives seven degrees of humility, the first of which is to acknowledge oneself contemptible; the second, to grieve for this; the third, to confess it; the fourth, to convince others of this, that is to wish them to believe it; the fifth, to bear patiently that this be said of us; the sixth, to suffer oneself to be treated with contempt; the seventh, to love being thus treated." Saint Thomas Aquinas, *Summa Theologica*, II-II q.161 a.6 obj. 3. We must consider, then, that the seven prayers are best understand corporately as a sign that John is writing to the Church Universal as a means to walk the great labyrinth of faith through seven communions with God.

The First Degree: Spiritual Gluttony

Spiritual Gluttony is the name St. John of the Cross gives to those individuals who fall into sin *because* of spiritual discipline. We see something like that in Ephesus. They *knew* the right ways and who were truly apostles and prophets. They *knew* enough to not tolerate wickedness, but in the end, their conscious knowledge of morals and ethics gave them such an ego they allowed their knowledge, and perhaps quest of perfection in the congregation, to separate themselves away from God. How? Their focus became themselves. They sought to perfect one another, rather than to allow God to perfect them.

> Many beginners, delighting in the sweetness and joy of their spiritual occupations, strive after spiritual sweetness rather than after pure and true devotion, which is that which God regards and accepts in the whole course of the spiritual way. For this reason, over and above their imperfection in seeking after sweetness in devotion, that spirit of gluttony, which has taken possession of them, forces them to overstep the limits of moderation, within which virtue is acquired and consists.[7]

It is difficult to remain on the middle ground, not too spiritually pure and not too spiritually impure. Perhaps penance can best be used to remind us of humility. If we continue with our prayers and strengthen them by adding to them small petitions or small adorations then we remember the One who is above us and it is from he we must receive grace. If penance is for the removal of sins by our hands, then we will forget Christ because we will come to think of ourselves as making the sacrifice rather than relying on the Cross for the once and future sacrifice. However, if penance consists of reminders, confessions and the ever-prodding walk to perfection, we may avoid the warning to the Ephesians.

---

7. Saint John of the Cross, *The Dark Night of the Soul*, 340.

The Second Prayer: Revelation 2:8–11

Lord, let us confess our sins to you,
We are like the Church of Smyrna
Let us heed the words of the one who was dead but now lives

Lord, you know our poverty and oppression
But you have called us rich
You know those who claim to be like us but insult us
They are not yours, but the dragon's
Let us not tremble at the things to come, but stand strong

O Lord, we are imprisoned, tested, and oppressed
But, we will remain faithful to you, even to our own death
Give us then the crown of life

O God, speak to us with the Spirit
Let us heed your promise to be victorious
In your victory, we will not face the second death

Amen

The Second Degree: In Poverty, Wealth

St. Clement, the third Bishop of Rome, wrote,

> Let our whole body, then, be preserved in, Christ Jesus; and let every one be subject to his neighbor, according to the special gift bestowed upon him. Let the strong not despise the weak, and let the weak show respect unto the strong. Let the rich man provide for the wants of the poor; and let the poor man bless God, because He hath given him one by whom his need may be supplied. Let the wise man display his wisdom, not by [mere] words, but through good deeds. Let the humble not bear testimony to himself, but leave witness to be borne to him by another. Let him that is pure in the flesh not grow proud of it, and boast, knowing that it was another who bestowed on him the gift of continence.[8]

---

8. 1 Clement 38.2 in *ANF*, 1:115.

It is up to the Son to take what *he* considers worthy and bring it as a gift before the Father. Jesus is the one speaking the words to remind them their poverty is wealth to God and their oppression freedom to the Father. In the Epistle to the Hebrews the author regularly paints an image of Jesus acting as High Priest in Heaven's Temple. It is not a difficult to see one of the sacrifices Jesus brings to his God is the sacrifice of the Smyrna Church.

Notice the paradox. When they were oppressed and accused, even murdered as seems to be the intention here, Jesus provides life. Why? "When the unlearned or unbeliever hears us sing triumphant songs to God for our victory over death, when he hears holy Lessons and discourses of the resurrection, when he hears us pray for a happy and joyful resurrection to Glory: by all these he must be convinced, that we do believe the resurrection, which is a principal Article of Christian faith, and the same may be the means to convince him also, and make him believe the same, and so fall down and worship God."[9]

What do these momentary trials do for the Christian? "Blessed is that soul which knows how to fight against the beast with seven heads, which he opposes to the seven degrees of love… And, beyond all doubt, if the soul shall faithfully fight against every one of these heads and obtain the victory, it will deserve to pass on from one degree to another, or from one mansion to the next, until it shall have reached the highest, having destroyed the seven heads by which the beast waged so furious a war against it."[10] God seeks to bring about our perfection! The great labyrinth of faith is not meant to trick us nor to ridicule us as a master might to a slave, or one child to another, but to strengthen us and to bring us up to heaven. If we suffer our pains as spiritual cowards, blaming God for our blights, what use is it to us? Better yet, suffer poverty cheerfully, and by poverty I mean whatever may work against you, and continue to move on.

---

9. Evans and Wright, *The Anglican Tradition*, 222.
10. Saint John of the Cross, *The Ascent of Mount Carmel*, 109–10.

The Penitential Prayer

The Third Prayer: Revelation 2:12–17

Lord, let us confess our sins to you,
We are like the Church of Pergamum
Speak to us by the sword of your mouth, O Lord

We live where the Dragon rules
But we hold high your banner
We will not deny our faith in you, O Lamb Slain
Even in the midst of oppression, we will be faithful

O Lord, cleanse from us those things you have against us
Let us not sell your message
Let us not bring others to shame by your word
Let us turn from the lust of the Dragon's throne to you
O Lord, we will put away our idols and our sins
Where we have conquered, give freedom and rebuke us
We repent; do not give us your wrath!

O God, speak to us with the Spirit
Let us heed your promise to be victorious
Feed us with the manna from heaven
Give us a new name, O Lord, known only to you.

Amen

The Third Degree: The Right Word

Once more we have entered into the ebb of the Spirit. While we have felt the joy of God's blessing like Smyrna, we are suffering a warning once more. This time, we are warned against teaching a false message that leads others into sin.

> We therefore, the interpreters of God's holy word, and faithful ministers of the church of Christ, must have a diligent regard to keep the scriptures sound and perfect, and to teach the people of Christ the word of God sincerely;

made plain, I mean, and not corrupted or darkened by foolish and wrong expositions of our own invention.[11]

Take a moment to examine what you teach in the name of God. Is it wholesome or simply filling? There are right doctrines if taught improperly may lead to ruin. Perhaps we do not speak well about our Christian faith. Does this matter today? Surely it does. While we do not all need proper education in theological dramas, we must be careful we do not waste either our time or those who listen to us by repeating error.

Another way to consider this prayer is to consider the reward for proper teaching. The hidden manna of 2:17 should be considered the bread of the Eucharist of which John in the Gospel assures us in Christ (John 6:25–58), but equally so, bread is the word of God (Luke 4:1–4; cf., Deuteronomy 8:3). If both are true, then the hidden manna is the teachings of and about Christ. We can, like yeast and flour, join these two elements—the Word of God, Jesus, and the words of God as contained in Scripture and the creeds of the Church—to give us hidden manna.

Thomas à Kempis adds, "Let our chief effort, therefore, be to study the life of Jesus Christ. The teaching of Christ is more excellent than all the advice of the saints, and he who has His spirit will find in it a hidden manna."[12] If we are able to overcome not just false teaching, but our inability to teach orthodox statutes, we will grow in perfection towards Christ (Ephesians 4:9–13). But, take care, "What good does it do to speak learnedly about the Trinity if, lacking humility, you displease the Trinity? Indeed it is not learning that makes a man holy and just, but a virtuous life makes him pleasing to God."[13] What does à Kempis mean? If in our learning we do not learn grace and virtue we are nothing more than Balaam and like the Church at

---

11. As found in Ritzema, *300 Quotations for Preachers from the Reformation*. Adapted from Henry Bullinger, *The Decades of Henry Bullinger*, 74–75.

12. à Kempis, *The Imitation of Christ*, 1.

13. à Kempis, *The Imitation of Christ*, 1–2.

Ephesus. While we have the right doctrines, our doctrines must lead to a good life (Ephesians 4:17–32).

Finally, Wesley expounds, "It seems properly to mean, the full, glorious, everlasting fruition of God."[14] Pray not just for wisdom, but also for the self-control to put the wisdom into action and not to lead anyone away from Jesus into the vain pursuit of knowledge without care.

The Fourth Prayer: Revelation 2.18–29

Lord, let us confess our sins to you,
We are like the Church of Thyatira
Why do you stand above us, O Lord
Your eyes are ablaze with fire and your feet bronze
Do you know of our love and faithfulness?
O God, remember our work and our patience
Watch as we grow in grace

Lord, we repent of false teachings
For we have welcomed into our midst one who tempts us away
We have given a place to idols and gone astray
We have not demanded repentance but now you do
Leave us not on a bed of pain
We renounce these teachings
Save us from your wrath

Reward us not for the false works we have done
We repent, O Searcher of Our Hearts and Minds
We will reject false teachings
We desire only the deep things of God
Give us no further burden, O Lord
We will remain faithful to you

O God, speak to us with the Spirit
Let us heed your promise to be victorious
We will endure to the end

14. Wesley, *Explanatory Notes Upon the New Testament*, 689.

> Our endurance will bring about authority over the nations
> They will be ruled with a rod of iron
> Give us the star of the morning, O Lord!

Amen

The Fourth Degree: An Exasperated God

> If we saw God, and heaven, and hell before us, do you think it would not effectually reconcile our differences, and heal our unbrotherly exasperations and divisions? Would it not hold the hands that itch to be using violence against those that are not in all things of their minds? What abundance of vain controversies would it reconcile! As the coming in of the master does part the fray among the schoolboys, so the sight of God would frighten us from contentious or uncharitable violence.[15]

G.K. Chesterton tells a story to a young man who is weary of the fight. "'But if,' I said, 'you picture to yourself that you are pulling against some powerful and oppressive enemy, the struggle will become merely exciting and not exasperating. Imagine that you are tugging up a lifeboat out of the sea. Imagine that you are roping up a fellow-creature out of an Alpine crevasse. Imagine even that you are a boy again and engaged in a tug-of-war between French and English.'"[16] I imagine this is how God is with us sometimes.

We have not yet learned our lesson from Pergamum. We had false teachers, and maybe we were false teachers, but instead of following God's instructions we continue our course and these problems multiply. There is nothing else to do but to wait on God to arrive. We have to repent even more profusely because now many of our leaders are the false teachers!

---

15. Adapted from Baxter, *The Practical Works of the Rev. Richard Baxter: Volume XII*, 43.
16. Chesterton, *All Things Considered*, 35–36.

Jesus stands off in the distance, waiting to hear us repent and profess our desire for the deep things of God. Not all things proposed as a revelation from God are really from God. We have seen this maltreatment of God with each generation. Neither is it new when great masses of people swell the ranks of the apostates. What is always newly re-discovered, however, is the safe harbor of the Church. When we return to the confines of a liberating doctrine and a liberating life of morality there we will see the deep things of God.

We have to ask ourselves when we either approach or cordon off teachings and new discoveries, is there an anchor here to God? If all truth is God's truth, then all new truths will point back to God. We can safely examine human origins, even cosmology, without fear as we have it in our Scripture and Theology the anchor to God for these things.

However, if we approach a new teacher and find they would dispose of all things before them, we must be cautious. If we create a new doctrine or a new canon, we must be weary. The search for something new has destroyed many. If a teacher promises us a new morality, move away. If a teacher promises a religion free of the cross, leave. If God is for it, the matter will prove itself correct. Until then, "hold fast that which remains" and wait upon the Lord.

The Fifth Prayer: Revelation 3:1–6

Lord, let us confess our sins to you,
We are like the Church of Sardis
O Lord, you know what we have done
We have your name, but we are dead

Let us awake and strengthen what remains
We are near death and God has forgotten us
We will remember the Gospel as at the first and keep it
We repent, O Lord, of our dead works
We will awake; do not come and remove our angel
Lord, like Abraham and Lot, grant us but a few to avert your wrath
Surely some of us walk with you as worthy followers

> O God, speak to us with the Spirit
> Let us heed your promise to be victorious
> Those who walk with you will be clothed in white
> Their names will be found in the book of life
> O Lamb, confess our names to your Father before the angels
>
> Amen.

The Fifth Degree: The Living Dead

"The contemporary demand for social justice . . . and much else on the secular agenda presuppose the universal and permanent dignity of man as man."[17] What does it matter if we but follow the social justice teachings of our respective denominations or communions? Would Jesus be unhappy? Perhaps. We could rely on Matthew 25 for the only creed worth repeating, but did the mission of Jesus end with feeding the earthly poor? If we rest completely on justice stances of Jesus, where is the Christ of Easter? If the conscious of the mind is not transformed, what is social justice but dead works? If we have no real and lasting faith, then our works are not enlivened, but remain only the works of a human hand.

> The fact that such a method of apologetics as that which we have been discussing should be advocated by learned and thoroughly loyal Churchmen proves that a grave state of tension exists between faith and reason. But Liberal Catholicism, as represented by the Abbé Loisy, surrenders far too much . . . It saves the Creeds, but loses the Gospels; it emancipates the will, but loses the intellect. It will be an evil day when the troubled faith of English Churchmen seeks refuge by this road.[18]

Sardis was a wealthy city with a troubled history. It was crushed beneath a massive earthquake and only rebuilt with the aid of Emperor Tiberius. Historically, it was dead, but because an emperor

---

17. Henry, *God, Revelation, and Authority*, 147.
18. William Ralph Inge, as discussed in Chapman, *The Coming Crisis*, 52.

chose, it remained alive. What sort of life was this? It had the trappings of its former glory, but after losing a bid to build a temple to the Roman ruler, it started to shrink, remaining important only out of necessity. When Christ speaks to it, he speaks to the hidden reality everyone knows but ignores.

The same is said of many of our churches today. They are simply dead while yet professing life. They worship the one true living God, but in what way? Have they not forsaken the Christian tradition and communion in order to do what they think is good? This does not apply to all, for many believe dwell within the Christian tradition by simply doing good. Yet, the whole of Tradition tells us what is required is a belief in God proper first. Thus the Creeds speak of our collective belief in the Holy Trinity. While many of us profess a level of belief, what this prayer is encouraging us to do is to awake to the reality of unbelief.

Has not the Christian Church, especially in the West, become little more than atheism with Christian trappings? "On the other hand, ideological rejection of God and an atheism of indifference, oblivious to the Creator and at risk of becoming equally oblivious to human values, constitute some of the chief obstacles to development today."[19] When we object to the God we find in Scripture, we are rejecting God on (our) ideological grounds. So, while we claim some right to be called a Christian and thus alive, we are little more than death waiting to be recognized. Rather than mystery, we return to the materialism of Epicurus.

The Sixth Prayer: Revelation 3:7–13

Lord, let us confess our sins to you,
We are like the Church of Philadelphia
You, O Lord, are holy and true
O My Jesus, you have the key of David
Shut the door so that none may open

19. Benedict XVI, *Caritas in Veritate*.

Lord, you know our deeds
You have given us an open door no one can shut
What power we have, you have given
We keep your words and hold fast your name

Lord, those who pretend to be like us but aren't,
Humble them so that they will know you love us
We keep the word of your promise; keep us from trials
Tempt not us, but try the world
Come quickly, O Lord, so that no one takes our crown!

O God, speak to us with the Spirit
Let us heed your promise to be victorious
Lord, you have promised to make us a pillar in the temple of your God
We will be at home, and will be marked with the name of your God
We will be at home, in the New Jerusalem, the city of your God

Amen

The Sixth Degree: The (Nearly) Open Door

The door is set before us, but it is not yet open.

In ancient temples, a *cella* was a small room placed in the temple to act as a door for the local god to come and go. In ancient churches, it is the place where the liturgy is directed. We should speak of the Eucharist table as that open door. As these prayers are meant for a penance to take us to the ultimate beatific vision of God, we should consider this open door *set* out for us. This reminds us we can approach the table not by our own strength (Zechariah 4:6), but by Christ who draws all of us (John 12:32–33).

> We set before these an open door of hope: Let them go in and give thanks unto the Lord; let them know that "the Lord is gracious and merciful, longsuffering, and of great goodness." "Look how high the heavens are from the earth! so far will he set their sins from them." "He will not always be chiding; neither keepeth he his anger for ever."

The Penitential Prayer

Only settle it in your heart, *I will give all for all*, and the offering shall be accepted. Give him all your heart! Let all that is within you continually cry out, "Thou art my God, and I will thank thee; thou art my God, and I will praise thee." "This God is my God for ever and ever! He shall be my guide even unto death."[20]

Wesley sees an open door for those whom he calls backsliders. Perhaps this is the best way to approach the Table of Christ, as a sinner in need of repair. We must first understand what this repair is, however. "The prayer of the man Jesus is now united with the dialogue of eternal love within the Trinity. Jesus draws men into this prayer through the Eucharist, which is thus the ever-open door of adoration and the true Sacrifice, the Sacrifice of the New Covenant, the 'reasonable service of God.'"[21] The communion table, to be taken from those properly designed to consecrate it as representatives of Jesus, is a medical table, filled with healing balm for our wounded souls.[22]

Finally, if Christ places before us this table, we must come to understand the communion table, our *cella*, is the center of worship. It is the access to God Christ in the Trinity has provided us. While the ancient people of God had a singular place of worship, located in one designated area, the modern people of God has a singular place, found not in a geographical locale, but where the proper priests of God assemble.

---

20. Wesley, *Sermons*, Sermon 86.
21. Ratzinger, *The Spirit of the Liturgy*, 49.
22. To add to the thesis of a Eucharist in view, compare 1 Corinthians 11:26 with Revelation 3:11 and the promise of Christ in 3:10 with Paul's hope for the Eucharist (1 Corinthians 11:28–32).

The Seventh Prayer: Revelation 3:14–22

Lord, let us confess our sins to you,

We are like the Church of Laodicea
O My Jesus, you are the Amen, the faithful and true Witness,
You are the Beginning of the creation of God

You know our lukewarm works
From you we hide
We confess that we are too wealthy to need you
We are too comfortable to pity you
We are warm to fear the cold and too cold to be exhausted
We labor not, but reap that which is labored for
We know everything and yet, O Lord, know nothing.
We fear we are still but poor, blind, and miserable sinners

We desire your gold, Great God, refined by your fire
We desire your fine linen and your oil
Let us see with your anointing.

O God, speak to us with the Spirit
Let us heed your promise to be victorious

Those you love, you rebuke.
We repent, O Lord, of our sins
Stand, knock. We will hear and will invite you in
Come, dine with us, O Lord
Plant us in your Father's house

Amen

The Seventh Degree: Neither

Let us turn again to St. John of the Cross,

> The Grace of God, like a loving mother, as soon as the soul is regenerated in the new fire and fervour of His service, treats it in the same way; for it is then furnished, without labour on its own part, with spiritual milk, sweet and

delicious, in the things of God, and in devotional exercises with great delight; God giving to it the breasts of His own tender love, as a mother to her babe. Such souls, therefore, delight to spend many hours, and perhaps whole nights, in prayer; their pleasures are penances, their joy is fasting, and their consolations are the use of the Sacraments and the frequentation of Divine Offices.[23]

"There is actually no direct ancient testimony for the inference that the water was tepid."[24] The author concludes his study by stating it was not the temperature of the water meant to be the focus, but the out of place abundance of bad water. The city of Laodicea had hot water while the city below had cold water. There was little temperature change by the time it reached our city, so the mystery here is not about the mellowness of the water. Instead, we know from other historical sources the area surrounding the city had an *abundance* of water, but that it was simply undrinkable. It was mixed with elements that became poisonous to the person. What is meant in this passage is not a condemnation of the lukewarm works of the people, but their belief in false self-sufficiency. It is this false water that should be compared, at least in the mind of the reader, to the living water of Christ provided through the Spirit. Further, this language, especially in 3:20, reveals the event that brings ultimate healing of our spiritual blindness.

In the ancient Church, baptism was not a momentary act made on the evening of a revival filled with emotional appeals but a process decided upon by both Church and Catechumen. Indeed, it centered on Easter and represented more than a decision to publicly profess "Jesus is Lord." Part of the ritual was to include white garments (3:18).[25]

23. St. John of the Cross, *The Dark Night of the Soul*, 327–28.
24. Hemer, *The Letters to the Seven Churches of Asia in Their Local Setting*, 189.
25. Rausch, *Catholicism in the Third Millennium*, 89. We cannot too easily separate what came first—Revelation's white garments or the baptismal garments. No doubt, they are intimately related.

To step back for a moment, Christ promises us three things in this passage—gold, white garments and healing medicine for the eyes. While the white garments are the baptismal robes, we are left to speculate about the refined gold? This is the act of repentance and refinement.[26] What then is the salve? Is it not, as Paul experienced, the removal of eyes of flesh in order to truly see Jesus by the Holy Spirit? Once we have repented, we are then able to take the Eucharist, the act we cannot do for ourselves.

These steps of penance are leading us to the beatific vision beginning immediately with the next chapter. We must see the Eucharist in full view in these letters. It is extremely noticeable in the last two churches. The table is set in the Philadelphia Church, but the image is completed in Laodicea when Christ says he will eat with us. This is the complete view of the Eucharist and the mystical way of experiencing Christ. "We must take seriously the Biblical doctrine of the Real Presence of Christ in the sacrament of the Eucharist. We must return to the Biblical pattern of worship centered on *Jesus Christ*, which means the weekly celebration of the Lord's Supper, as well as instruction about its true meaning . . . In Holy Communion we are genuinely having dinner with Jesus, lifted up into His heavenly presence; and, moreover, we are feasting on Him."[27]

The mystic speaks to the regeneration of the soul, regenerated by something new. In our Christian life, it is assured we will suffer something of decay from the initial zeal. Perhaps we will even become an atheist for a while, deciding it is easier and more rational to not believe in a God than it is to suppose the universe does in fact have a beginning and an end ordained by Something. We should not disparage anyone who is suffering either under the initial fire of salvation or those who have suffered a lack of oxygen and thus have seen their flame extinguished. Instead, we should hope always for a new life in our march to perfection.

---

26. See Psalm 66:10; Zechariah 13:9; and Isaiah 1:25

27. Chilton, *The Days of Vengeance*, 138. See also Barber, *Coming Soon*, 74–76.

This is not to say we desire something new every day, else we would appear rather insatiable in our desire and thus ungrounded. Instead, we must seek the Spirit's move, which like waves and wind, ebbs and flows. This ebb allows us to experience doubt and fear and prepares us for a turn to faith and security. The people at Laodicea saw their church dying. It was stuck somewhere in the middle, doing only what it was supposed to do. But God demands more than simply following rules.

3

The Beatific Vision

"(John) sees a door in heaven ... it is promised the heavenly mysteries are to be opened to him because Christ is the door."[1]

Teresa of Avila once wrote,

> To think then we shall enter heaven without praying, and entering into ourselves by the knowledge of ourselves and the consideration of our own misery, and what we owe to God, and by often imploring His mercy, is foolishness. Our Lord himself has said, "No one can come to the Father, but by me;" and somewhere else He says, "He that seeth me, seeth the Father also." Now, if we never look at Him, nor consider how much we owe Him, nor the death He suffered for us, I do not understand how we can know Him, or perform works in His service; for what value can faith have without these, and what worth can these have, if not united with the merits of Christ? Neither do I know who can excite us to love this Lord. May His Majesty be pleased to make us know how dearly we have cost Him, and that "the servant is not greater than the master," and that we must *work* in order to enjoy His glory, and for this

---

1. Venerable Bede, *The Explanation of the Apocalypse*.

reason we must pray likewise, that so we may not fall into temptation.[2]

Might we turn into ourselves to examine if we are in the right frame of mind for prayer? We have seen Jesus introduced to us in chapter 1 and prayed the prayers of repentance with the churches in Asia. Are we not yet ready to see if we may yet meet God? And if we see God, what might we ask of him? 1 Kings 3 tells the story of Solomon's petition for wisdom. Solomon had spiritually divested himself of his other wants and care to consider not what was best for himself, physically or emotionally, but for the betterment of others. If we pray for riches or fame, perhaps even for health, our spiritual attention is not God, but ourselves.[3] Unless we can devoid ourselves of these things, we may never see God.

> For this it is necessary to make ourselves indifferent to all created things in all that is allowed to the choice of our free will and is not prohibited to it; so that, on our part, we want not health rather than sickness, riches rather than poverty, honor rather than dishonor, long rather than short life, and so in all the rest; desiring and choosing only what is most conducive for us to the end for which we are created.[4]

Are you prepared to meet God? "Therefore the *mystic* prays in thought during every hour, being by love allied to God. And first he will ask forgiveness of sins; and after, that he may sin no more; and further, the power of well-doing and of comprehending the whole creation and administration by the Lord, that, becoming pure in

---

2. Saint Teresa of Ávila, *The Interior Castle*, 25. Perhaps we might sum up the first line as, "how foolish is it to consider entering heaven without first entering into ourselves."

3. There are several books dedicated to using Revelation as a guide to attain some sort of financial windfall, serving to show just how poorly the authors misunderstand the goal not just of Revelation, but likewise the Gospel.

4. Saint Ignatius of Loyola, *The Spiritual Exercises of St. Ignatius of Loyola*, 19.

heart through the knowledge, which is by the Son of God, he may be initiated into the beatific vision face to face, having heard the Scripture which says, 'Fasting with prayer is a good thing.'"[5]

First Prayer: Revelation 4:1–11

Look up!
See a door standing open in heaven,
Hear the voice John hears speaking as a trumpet blast.
The voice says,
"Come up here to me, and I will reveal to you what is taking place."

God takes his place in the divine council of the cherubim
In the midst of the gods his judgment is given[6]

Dwell in the Spirit —
Behold!
Do you see the throne in heaven
Do you see the one sitting there?

Our Pride fills us
We see the Lord sitting high on his throne
The hem of his robe fills the temple
If we but touch the hem, we will be healed

The six-winged Seraphim attend him
With two they covered their faces,
With two they covered their feet
But with two, they fly
Hear as one calls to another saying:

"Holy, holy, holy is the LORD of hosts—
"Holy, holy, holy, the whole earth is full of his glory."

---

5. Clement of Alexandria, *The Stromata*, XII in *ANF*, 2:503. I have changed the word *gnostic* to *mystic* because this is what Clement would say today. I was confirmed in this after a private conversation with Clementine scholar, Rodney Thomas, who has written his thesis on the subject.

6. The refrain comes from Psalm 82:1. John is beckoned to the divine council, as we are in our prayers.

The Beatific Vision

Behold our God sits on a throne of jasper and carnelian
The glow of a circle like coal burning surrounded his throne like a rainbow.

Let the coal burn our lips and sin be blotted out

Twenty-four thrones surrounded him
Twenty-four elders sit there.
They are clothed in white and have gold crowns.

These are the priests in the heavenly Temple
They offer to our God continuously

From the Throne are sounding
Flashes of lightning and the peals of thunder
Before the Throne are standing
Seven torches with a consuming fire

We behold the sevenfold Spirit of God.

In front of the throne is a shiny sea of glass of crystal
In the center and around the throne are four living beings
Each beast is covered with eyes, front and back
The first of these is like a lion
The second an ox
The third has a human face
The fourth flies like the eagle.

We ask, "How long, O Lord?"

The thresholds shook at the voices of those who called,
The house fills with smoke

He says to us
"Until cities lie waste without inhabitant,
Until houses without people,
Until the land is utterly desolate;
Until the LORD sends everyone far away
Until the land is void and without form."[7]

---

7. Isaiah 6:1–13.

Each of these living beings had six wings,
Their wings were covered all over with eyes, inside and out.
Day after day and night after night they sing,
"Holy, holy, holy is the Lord God, the Almighty
He is was, is, and is still to come."

"How long will you judge unjustly and show partiality to the wicked?
Give justice to the weak and the orphan!
Preserve the right of the lowly and the destitute."

Do you see the living ones giving glory
And honor and thanks to the one sitting on the throne
He is the one who lives forever and ever,

Rescue the tired and the destitute
Deliver them from the hand of the perverse
They have neither knowledge nor understanding
They trod around in darkness

The twenty-four elders fall down
They worship the one sitting on the throne
He is the one who lives forever and ever
The elders place their crowns before the throne and say,

We hear God saying
"All of you are gods, children of the Most High;
However, you will die like mortals,
And collapse like any prince."

But we say,
"You are worthy, O Lord our God, to have glory
And honor and power
For you formed all things
They exist because you it pleased you."

But we say,
"Rise up, O God, and bring justice to the earth;
Remember all the nations of this earth belong to you![8]

Amen

8. Psalm 82:2–8.

The Beatific Vision

"Every Lord's day is a day of rest, but this, perhaps, more than any. It commemorates, not an act of God, however gracious and glorious, but His own unspeakable perfections and adorable mysteriousness. It is a day especially sacred to peace… Christ here says, that instead of this world's troubles, He gives His disciples peace; and, accordingly, in to-day's Collect, we pray that we may be kept in the faith of the Eternal Trinity in Unity, *and* be 'defended from all adversities,' for in keeping that faith we are kept from trouble."[9] Thus says Cardinal Newman about Sunday, the Lord's Day. It is not simply the day Jesus rose from the grave, but so too the eighth day of creation when God's work begins. It is a day filled with promise and a day meant to foreshadow the ultimate Sabbath when we are given our final rest with God.

There is something of an interplay between John's magnificent imagery of the worshiping of our God in Revelation 4, the prophet's heavenly vision after the death of King Uzziah in Isaiah 6, and the Psalmist's revelation of the heavenly throne in the Psalm 82. They fit neatly together in most places; however, there is the Prophet's idea of justice, something I believe we often wish to see—the death of our enemies. We call this justice. We desire a vengeful god bent to our desires, to inflict pain and suffering and such as we have had from our enemies we demand he gives to them.

In Isaiah 6, YHWH calls for a prophet to go and speak for him. Isaiah readily answers, but he finds his lips are just as unclean as the people's. God sees this too, placing a burning coal to singe away the impurities of the flesh. When John sees the Great Throne of God in his vision, it is surrounded by fiery coal. Scripture does not tell us John has his sins blotted out by the coal—and why should it? John is a disciple of Jesus, after all. Instead, the coal reminds us both of Isaiah and that fire is no longer needed for a sacrifice (Mark 9:38–50).

---

9. Newman, *Parochial and Plain Sermons, Volume 6*, 362–63.

Praying in God's Theater

In the Psalm 82, the poet crafts the scene of YHWH standing victorious among the other gods now paying him homage. It is difficult for us today, with our developed view of monotheism, to allow for gods and lords, but Scripture teaches us to worship the Most High God, not to deny the existence of other gods (1 Corinthians 5:8). We might allow these gods to be angels and/or demons. That is what Justin Martyr, a second century Christian apologist believed. The angels, gods, or maybe even demons stand and bow to the Most High God. All others stand defeated in the death of Christ.

How might we understand these gods and lords abounding throughout Scripture and the early Apologists? Might we turn to the allegorical, drawing upon the richness of metaphor? Indeed we should. If we identify the gods in our daily lives would we not see them in competition with Christ? The gods and other lords in our lives are those things luring us away from proper worship. They can possess us at any time, even if we are sitting before the table of the Lord. They can inhabit our family lives, our work places, and even our alone time. These are the distractions, natural and unnatural, preventing the fullness of the promise of the Gospel.

I have intermixed these three passages together to give a picture of the heavenly God ill respondent to the cares of his creation, not as a slight, but because we must often feel this way. How else do we make sense of the tragedies of genocide, starvation, and poverty? Perhaps God is too surrounded by adoration to notice us? Perhaps it is, as we are too often told, our sins keeping God from hearing our prayers. Placing these three passages together calls attention to the force of this prayer, to call God's attention away from the adoring throng of the vanquished gods to the injustices we have yet to conquer. We demand of God justice on earth.

Did John really see this? Ian Boxall writes, "What is most surprising about these parallel accounts is their relative lack of verbal agreement with each other . . . contrary to what one might expect were one dealing with literary borrowing. Rather, the fluidity of language, and the piling up of similes and metaphors to express what is seen, may point us in the direction of actual visionary experience on the part of their authors."[10] While it may be difficult to imagine someone taking a physical heavenly or otherworldly journey, we can allow John believed he did take such a journey. It is possible to postulate such an event as taking place only in John's mind; however, we must ask ourselves "what is real?" We do have cases of mass hysteria causing visions or other social panics; yet this does not seem to accurately describe what is going on with John. We may attribute John's work to a "real" vision, although with some nuance.[11]

The open door is symbolic of our prayer and entry into the highest realms of reality. What is reality but that which is? God cannot exist outside of reality—apart from God, there is nothing else; therefore, God is the ultimate reality, although we may yet perceive the fullness of God. Through John we are beckoned to come through the open door and traverse both space and time to see reality from God's point of view. Here, John is presented with the totality of time—from the beginning of Creation to the beginning of the New. We must not think of time controlling reality, but of reality laying step after step for time to travel. This is the meaning of "afterwards I saw." John is pulled into the greater reality, into God, and escaping time.[12]

Why has the door remained closed? Perhaps it has not been closed, but simply we were unable to see it. Mystics have written of the door and of the other side with measured hope. However, John not only sees the door, but he is beckoned to ascend by Christ who has already ascended (John 3:13) when he defeated sin. Because of

---

10. Boxall, *The Revelation of Saint John*, 81.

11. "Real" is a rather subjective term. With the onset of Pentecostalism at the end of the nineteenth century, many have claimed the experience of speaking in tongues. Yet, anthropologists can compare this to other primitive religious rituals involving ecstatic utterances. We should not too hastily decide what is real and what is not based either on science or personal experiences. The theological notion of real presence fits into our discussion neatly and will be addressed later.

12. Tyconius writes, "The interval of time belongs not to the events but to the visions. If one were to describe a single event in different ways, it would be the descriptions that differ in time, not what took place at one time . . . (John) traces the whole span of the church" (*Commentary on the Apocalypse 4.1*).

this, John "ascends from the valley of tears to the height of dignity."[13] John's mind "turn(s) away completely from the things of the earth and be turned toward heaven."[14]

Thronos, Greek for throne, is used fourteen times in this chapter and over forty times in the entirety of John's work. "No matter what may happen on earth, God is on His throne and is in complete control. Various teachers interpret Revelation in different ways, but all agree that John is emphasizing the glory and sovereignty of God."[15] With John, we are able to get a first look at God's throne, something meant to be understood as placing John (and through John also the reader) into a most holy of fraternity. When we view God's throne, we are given the ability to dismiss idle and childish faith and with a mature faith come to understand God's sovereign control.

Twenty-four elders surround the throne. More than likely they represent the cyclical rotation of priests. "These orders were fixed in the Old Testament (1 Chronicles 24–25), continued in the New Testament period and were still commented on by later rabbis and in later inscriptions."[16] But the number is equally representative of several aspects of the Jewish and Christian traditions. First, the number may represent the books found in the Jewish canon, but this is unlikely, as the canon was not yet settled by the time Revelation was written. Second, it is possible these elders represent the union of the Twelve Tribes of Israel and the Twelve Apostles.

---

13. Primasius, *Commentary on the Apocalypse*, 4.1.
14. Andrew of Caesarea, *Commentary on the Apocalypse*, 4.1.
15. Wiersbe, *The Bible Exposition Commentary*, Rev. 4:1.
16. Keener, *The IVP Bible Background Commentary: New Testament*, Rev. 4:4. Keener goes on to write, "The faithful dead are thus portrayed as priests offering worship to God." What are we to make of the faithful dead attending to God's throne? As we will see later, they are very much accompanied with voice, thought, and presence.

A Prayer of Adoration

Silence our heart, O Lord
The door you have set before us,
The door is opened for us
Beckon us, Great God, to come to you
Show us what takes place where we cannot see

Stay, O Holy Spirit, with us always
Show us the throne and the One who sits there
Let us see for a moment the jasper stone
Reveal to us the sardius, the rainbow, and the emerald

Son of God, let us bow low and worship the Trinity
O Elders of the Temple, throw down your crowns
Worship the One True God

O God, our hearts tremble to see you
Our eyes are frightened and our soul fears
The lightening strikes and the thunder peals
Protect us by your Spirits

O Son of Man, let us read of you in the face of the four creatures
Behold the throne secured and worshiped by the Gospels Four
Behold the lion and the calf
See the man and the eagle
These tell us your story, O My Jesus

O Blessed Trinity,
Holy to the Father
Holy to the Son
Holy to the Holy Spirit
O Blessed Trinity, the Lord God, Almighty

Lord God, King of the Earth, we bow to you
Worthy are you, O Lord our God
Worthy are you to receive glory and honor and power
You are creator and we worship you.

4

The Presentation of the Gospel, Part I

> "O Lord our God, who lacks nothing, accept this incense offered by an unworthy hand, and deem us all worthy of Thy blessing, for Thou art our sanctification, and we ascribe glory to Thee."[1]

The totality of the Christian faith is built on Jesus Christ, the Lamb of God who was slain to take away the sins of the world (John 1.29). To this we add his divine status, the resurrection, the Church and so on. We must always begin with the role Jesus played. It is not merely that of a philosopher or teacher, but of the divine Son of God chosen by the Father to wage a holy war against the kingdoms of this earthly plane and thereby bring salvation from eternity to all. While we may quibble still yet how best to describe this—is it the Substitutionary Atonement or is it *Christus Victor*?—what matters is not our proper words or correct understanding but the reality of the event itself.

By now, we have passed through the stages of penance and stood at the door of heaven to see the beatific vision. With John we see the Lamb participating by his own hand in the salvation of the world.

---

1. An anaphora from one of the early liturgies as found in "*The Divine Liturgy of the Holy Apostle and Evangelist Mark*" in *ANF*, 7:554.

Why? According to developing Christian theological tradition as expressed by St. Paul the Law of Moses was insufficient to present us a lasting grace. This is why John weeps. He would have known nothing before was sufficient to save the souls of the human race. But, it was efficient in bringing shame to us only alleviated by the death of Jesus.

The First Prayer: Revelation 5:1–8

A scroll is in the right hand of the one who was sitting on the throne.
There is writing on the inside
And the outside of the scroll
It is sealed with seven seals.

The Prophet Daniel was commanded
Keep his prophecy a secret
Seal up the book until the time of the end
Many will rush here and there
Knowledge will increase.[2]

See the strong angel
He shouts with a loud voice,
"Who is worthy to break the seals on this scroll and open it?"
Why does our heart break?

The Lord declares
Return to me with all your heart
Return with fasting and lamentation and remembrance.
Return to the Lord our God,
He is gracious and compassionate
He is measured in anger and abounding in love
Will he surrender from sending catastrophe?
May he repent and leave us a blessing.
Blow the trumpet in Zion
We declare a holy fast
Let the Church be assembled![3]

2. Daniel 12:4.
3. Joel 2:12–16.

Praying in God's Theater

We see no one in heaven
Or on earth
Or under the earth able to open the scroll
We are inconsolable
No one is worthy to open the scroll.

**Let the ministers of the Lord weep in the sanctuary
Let them cry out, "Spare your people, Lord!
If the seal is not opened, the Lord's inheritance will become nothing—
An object of scorn
A relic of the past
A forgotten tomb among other graves
Other gods will ask, "Where is your God?"**[4]

Hear the elders around the throne saying,
"Cease mourning!
Behold the Lion of the tribe of Judah,
Behold the heir to David's throne
Behold Christ the Victor!
He alone is worthy to open the scroll and its seven seals."

**Gather the people!
Adorn the Church!
Gather the ministers!
Gather the children!
The Bridegroom Comes
Await the Bride!**

See the Lamb once slaughtered
But now stands between the throne, the four beasts, and the elders.
He has seven horns and seven eyes
He has the sevenfold Spirit of God
He is sent out into every part of the earth.

**We praise the Lamb slain!
For you are our glory and strength
By your grace you lift up our soul!**

4. Joel 2:17.

The Presentation of the Gospel, Part I

We belong to the Lord,
He is our king!
The Lord is the King of the Holy One of Israel[5]

We watch in anticipation as the Lamb steps forward
We watch as the Lamb approaches the Father
Behold the Lamb as he takes the scroll from the right hand
From the right hand of God, the scroll is given to the Lamb Slain.

The Prophet saw a man dressed in linen,
Standing above the river, raising both hands toward heaven
A solemn oath by the one who lives forever the man takes,
"Pain and suffering and death and despair will happen.
But the crushing of the holy people has ended."[6]

The company of heaven falls down before the Lamb.
Each one has a harp,
Each hold gold vessels filled with incense,
These are the prayers of the people of God.

Our visions occupy our nights,
We see one like a son of man coming with the clouds of heaven.
He approaches the Ancient One
He leads into his presence.
He is given sovereignty over all the nations of the world
Babel is undone
His rule is eternal
His kingdom will never be destroyed.[7]
We occupy our visions this night

Amen

---

5. Psalm 89:17–18.
6. Daniel 12:7.
7. Daniel 7:13–14.

The New Exodus

The Torah motifs abound in this chapter. There is a new covenant represented by the seals. Jesus is pictured as the New Moses, the only one who can go into Egypt to redeem God's people. The songs in the Revelation 5 and 15 are likened to the Songs of Moses in Exodus 15 and Deuteronomy 32:1–43, causing us to consider Revelation as the totality of salvation's history. Consider this first—we are but repeating the story of Israel, only towards perfection. Consider this second—there is a New Covenant, a New Moses, even a New Exodus. We must have a new Tabernacle and a New Temple. Where is this? This is not merely when we assemble, but wherever the Table of the Lord is. What is the Exodus story without the Passover?

We see the trappings of a liturgical celebration.[8] There is the sacrifice (5:6), the priestly taking of Scripture (5:7), hymns of worship to God, and the incense offered with the prayers of the saints (5:8). Finally, there is the new song of the redeemed (5:9–10). We might see it organized as such today on Sunday mornings in a mirror of the divine. Beginning with Leviticus we are given examples of this such as when God gave the plans of the Tabernacle to Moses to mimic the heavenly realm. We know from Hebrews the sacrifice in heaven is connected to the sacrifice on earth. Matthew tells us the teachings of the Church must reflect that which is in Heaven (Matthew 16:18–9). Why do we find it too incredible to believe our reasonable worship is properly designed to be in concert with Heaven?

When we pray, we must not be so conceited as to think we are individuals. Indeed, we pray with the angels and the saints in heaven. In doing so we seek an earthly part of the heavenly worship. "The worship of Jesus as the sacrificial Lamb in Scripture is also analogous to Eucharistic adoration, in its rich Passover imagery."[9] As we have

---

8. I am not the first, nor the last, to see Revelation 4–5 as an early liturgy. The reality of this is discussed by Mowry in "Revelation 4–5 and Early Christian Liturgical Usage," 75–84.

9. Armstrong, *Biblical Catholic Answers for John Calvin*, 294.

seen, the connection of the heavenly to the earthly is through the Eucharist.

> He, therefore, that will go up into the mount of perfection and hold communion with God, must not only abandon everything, but restrain even his desires, the sheep and the cattle from feeding in sight of the mount—that is, upon anything which is not simply God, in Whom, that is, in the state of perfection, every desire must cease. This journey or ascent must therefore be a perpetual struggle with our desires to make them cease, and the more earnest we are the sooner shall we reach the summit. But until the desires cease we can never reach it, notwithstanding our many virtues, for virtue is not perfectly acquired before our souls are empty, detached, and purified from all desire.[10]

The mystic will know their individual imperfections and disabilities. They will know their moments of unworthiness. They will know these things about themselves even when no one else will. We are commanded to search ourselves (2 Corinthians 13:5), to see where we are with God. In the Old Testament, the Jews would search out their house to rid themselves of those things unacceptable during Passover. This is one of the hidden scenes in this drama unfolding before us. John knows he is not worthy to take part in the covenant with God. John, a co-worker with Jesus (Revelation 1:1), was still unworthy to receive the scroll. "Internal and external difficulties must not make us pessimistic or inactive. What counts, as in every area of Christian life, is the confidence that comes from faith, from the certainty that it is not we who are the principal agents of the Church's mission, but Jesus Christ and his Spirit. We are only co-workers and when we have done all that we can, we must say: 'We are unworthy servants; we have only done what was our duty.'"[11]

If there is a hidden mystery in this drama, it is the unspoken Eucharist. What else propels us in our life with Christ but the Table of

---

10. Saint John of the Cross, *The Ascent of Mount Carmel*, 24.
11. John Paul II, *Redemptoris Missio*.

the Lord? Wesley comments, "Consider the Lord's Supper, Secondly, as a mercy from God to man. As God, whose mercy is over all his works, and particularly over the children of men, knew there was but one way for man to be happy like himself; namely, by being like him in holiness; as he knew we could do nothing toward this of ourselves, he has given us certain means of obtaining his help. One of these is the Lord's Supper, which, of his infinite mercy, he hath given for this very end; that through this means we may be assisted to attain those blessings which he hath prepared for us; that we may obtain holiness on earth, and everlasting glory in heaven."[12]

Wesley goes further and speaks to those who reject the Table because they feel within themselves such an infirmity as to avoid even grace. He writes, "God offers you one of the greatest mercies on this side heaven, and commands you to accept it. Why do not you accept this mercy, in obedience to his command? You say, 'I am unworthy to receive it.' And what then? You are unworthy to receive any mercy from God. But is that a reason for refusing all mercy? God offers you a pardon for all your sins. You are unworthy of it, it is sure, and he knows it; but since he is pleased to offer it nevertheless, will not you accept of it? He offers to deliver your soul from death: You are unworthy to live; but will you therefore refuse life? He offers to endue your soul with new strength; because you are unworthy of it, will you deny to take it? What can God himself do for us farther, if we refuse his mercy because we are unworthy of it?"[13]

While John—you and I—is unworthy to take, and thereby begin, the new covenant, we are not left hopeless. In order to participate in the new covenant, we must know our limitations, our sins, and then ascend to the Table in humility. It is what restores us to our ability to be a co-worker with Christ.

---

12. Wesley, *Sermons*, Sermon 101.
13. Wesley, *Sermons*, Sermon 101.

The Presentation of the Gospel, Part I

The Second Prayer: Revelation 5:9–14

Sing a new song with these words!

He has given us a new song to sing
A new hymn of praise to our God is on our tongue.
Let the multitudes see what God has done
Let them now put their trust in the Lord.[14]

Hear what our God says,
"You are worthy to take the scroll
You are worthy to break open the seals
For you were slain, O Lamb!
It is your blood ransoming all people for God
You initiated the Kingdom of priests
They will reign on the earth."

The Apostle Peter says
Because you have had a taste of the Lord's kindness
Be like newborns
Crave pure spiritual milk
Grow into the full experience of salvation.
Cry out for this sustenance,
Come to Christ,
He is the living cornerstone of God's temple.
The people rejected him
God chose him
God now chooses us
Through the reconciliation of Jesus Christ,
We offer spiritual sacrifices pleasing to God
We are living stones in God's spiritual temple
We are his holy priests.[15]

Look again and hear the voices of thousands and millions of angels
Hear the voices of creatures and the elders
They surround the throne with this new song

---

14. Psalm 40:3.
15. 1 Peter 2:2–5.

We watched as thrones are put in place
The Ancient One sat down to judge.
He sits on a fiery throne with wheels of blazing fire
His clothing was as white as snow
His hair like purest wool
A river of fire pours out, flowing with his presence.
The angels minister to him;
Millions stand to praise him.
The Court is ready—let the books be opened[16]

Hear the mighty chorus of angels
"Worthy is the Lamb slain
Worthy is he to receive the treasures of heaven and earth and every blessing."

You, O king, are a king of kings,
The God of heaven has given you a kingdom exceeding all measure[17]

Do you hear every creature singing?
"Blessing and honor and glory
Blessing and power belong to the one sitting on the throne
And to the Lamb forever and ever."
The four living creatures say, "Amen!"
The twenty-four elders fall down to worship the Lamb.

Praise the Lord with all that I am!
We are joyful because we have the God of Israel as our helper
Our hope is in the Lord our God.
He brings the cosmos to being.
His promises are always kept
He gives justice to the oppressed and feeds the hungry.
The Lord gives pardon to the captives.
The Lord opens the eyes of the blind.
The Lord lifts up the depressed.
The Lord loves the godly.
The Lord shelters the strangers.
The Lord cares for the orphans and widows

16. Daniel 7:9–10.
17. Daniel 2:37 LXX.

The Lord reigns forever.
The Lord is the God of Zion and Jerusalem forever.
Praise the Lord![18]

Amen

The New Song

> Behold the might of the new song! It has made men out of stones, men out of beasts. Those, moreover, that were as dead, not being partakers of the true life, have come to life again, simply by becoming listeners to this song. It also composed the universe into melodious order, and tuned the discord of the elements to harmonious arrangement, so that the whole world might become harmony. It let loose the fluid ocean, and yet has prevented it from encroaching on the land. The earth, again, which had been in a state of commotion, it has established, and fixed the sea as its boundary. The violence of fire it has softened by the atmosphere, as the Dorian is blended with the Lydian strain; and the harsh cold of the air it has moderated by the embrace of fire, harmoniously arranging these the extreme tones of the universe. And this deathless strain,—the support of the whole and the harmony of all,—reaching from the center to the circumference, and from the extremities to the central part, has harmonized this universal frame of things, not according to the Thracian music, which is like that invented by Jubal, but according to the paternal counsel of God, which fired the zeal of David.[19]

What are we to make of the new song? If Jesus is the Lamb slain before the foundation of the world—that is what we are seeing here—then the new song *is* the ultimate victory, our rescue from death, the very act salvation accomplishes.

---

18. Psalm 146:1, 5–10.
19. Clement of Alexandria, *Exhortation to the Heathen*, in *ANF,* 2:172.

"Thus, it is in the Liturgy of the Eucharist that Christ bestows the kingdom to the Church."[20] Notice the elements of the Exodus story *and* our modern liturgical celebrations in John's descriptive composition of the scene in Heaven. Where Moses once stood, Jesus now stands. Likewise, where Jesus now stands in heaven, our ministers are to stand in our Eucharistic celebrations. The song is not merely a hymn of worship, but the power by which we celebrate Jesus and Jesus infuses our communion with his presence. We see in our services that rightfully mirror the heavenly, the outpouring by Jesus of the Spirit through the new song.

New can mean renewed, as in quality. This is why we as Christians can seek to preserve the Jewish character of the Old Testament while yet renewing it through our spiritual ministry without the appearance of inept absconding of authorial intent. When we turn to the Psalms we see Moses playing a central role, especially in Psalms 90–100. In the Gospels, we see the Psalms playing a role in how Jesus speaks to his Father (I note the use of Psalm 22 when Christ is upon the cross). In Acts, Paul, and Hebrews the Holy Spirit speaks through the Psalms to bring the Church to a better understanding of who Jesus truly is. We should not easily forsake the past, but instead seek to use our foundation for what God has in store for us.

A Prayer of Adoration

> Great God, we see you on your throne
> The scroll of the seven seals is unopened
> Is no one worthy, O Lord, to open it?
> Must the mystery of the End remain always closed?
>
> O Lord, search Heaven and search Earth
> Is there not one who is worthy to look inside of it?
> Our God, have you forsaken your people to this fate?
> Are we without you finally?

---

20. Barber, *Coming Soon*, 93.

The Presentation of the Gospel, Part I

Lord, we hear you speaking to our hearts
We will not weep for we can see Judah's Lion,
We behold David's Son
He has overcome and is worthy to open the scroll
Hallelujah to the Lion of Judah's Tribe,
Praise to the King of Israel

You, O My Jesus, you alone are worthy to break the seal
You were slain for our transgressions
It is by your sacred blood you have redeemed for God a people
Your people now number endlessly and cover all
You make them a royal house of priest for God
They will reign on the earth because of you

O Lamb of God,
Let our voice join with those of the beasts, the elders, and the angels
Let our voice drawn in the sea of the redeemed multitude
We will proclaim with a loud voice that you are worthy
Jesus, you who were slain, receive power and peace
Receive wisdom and strength
Honor, glory, and praise belong only to you

Lord, our voice joins with the dead to sing your praises
Praise, honor, glory, and strength to who sits on the throne
Praise, honor, glory, and strength to the Lamb!
Let all of heaven and earth say 'amen'

A Prayer of Supplication

I cannot help but see this as a cry for the world. John knows the sin preventing God from just rescuing us, but also the love preventing God from simply condemning all of us. John knows the old covenant has not yet brought the fullness of the remission of sins. Perhaps that is why this chapter has taken the form of a New Exodus. But here, we pray as John—who sees the plagues on the world and laments that no one is worthy to stop it.

Who is worthy, Great God, to open the new covenant?
Who is holy to break the seals?
We weep because we are not worthy
Our sins are still with us, and we are unholy
We have searched our lives but can find no one
When then, O God, can you save us for we cannot save ourselves?

O Soul, cease your mourning,
See, O People, you King!
It is Jesus, the Lamb Slain for us
O My Jesus, you alone are worthy to save us!
Come Victor! Come and take the covenant!

Rise, my prayers, to the throne
Because now we are able through Jesus
Worthy are you, O Lamb of God Slain for us
Break the seals and read the book,
Covenant with us and take away our sin
Purchase us and redeem us with your blood
Undo Babel's curse and make us all one people
Make us priests to your God!

Worthy is the Lamb Slain!
Worthy are you to receive all power, grace, and honor
Holy are you to receive all glory and every blessing
Blessing and honor, glory and power forever to the one on the throne
And to the Lamb
Let our prayers be songs in the ears of God and his lamb

5

The Presentation of the Gospel, Part II

"This one animal is the whole church preaching with a great voice and inviting the church to greater faith, 'Come and see!' 'If anyone thirsts, let him come and drink.'"[1]

"The eschatological theme, taken on its own, is incomprehensible without the cadence of Christ's suffering. The vertical form of the Son of God who descends from the Father and goes back to him would be illegible without the horizontal form of historical fulfillment and of the mission entrusted to the Apostles."[2] Oecumenius is the author of the earliest Greek commentary on the Book of Revelation. His commentary is devoted to the concept of salvation history and it is no more clearly seen than in his chapter examining Revelation 6. For him and other early Christian writers Scripture was not simply the words on the page, but also the unsaid words before and after what appears to us by the hands of the prophets and apostles. When Oecumenius examines the passage of the four horsemen, his focus is not on the horses and their riders, but on the events causing

---

1. St. Primasius, as found in Weinrich, ed., *Revelation*, 82.
2. von Balthasar, *The Glory of the Lord*, 500.

the breaking of the seals. For him, everything is related directly to the Gospel.

"Let us again pray to the Lord in peace. Receive us, save us, and have pity on us, O Lord."[3] These horses represent prompts to remember the Gospel. If we were designing Revelation as an ancient liturgy, we might call this the *Oremus*—small prayers said by the congregation before the reading of the Scripture.

The latter part of Revelation 6 recounts the crucifixion using language familiar to passages drawn from Joel and Isaiah. If the last part of this chapter recounts the story of the crucifixion, might the first part tell of the Incarnation? Critics may allege a discrepancy here, as the Lamb Slain is already seen, but just as in Eucharistic celebrations and prayer, the lines of heaven and earth are erased in our vision. If we seek to tell again of the death, burial, and resurrection of Jesus in our liturgy, must we always remind our listeners we are starting over? No. The same can be said here of John, and the more so since John is moving from heaven to earth.

The Incarnation is a singular event in salvation history where the Son of God became human (Philippians 2:5–11). In Matthew and Luke, we see the process of the Incarnation as it begins on earth, but as we move into John, the Evangelist reports to us the scene from heaven, complete with the act of the Divine tabernacling–with–flesh (John 1:14). The lines between heaven and earth become muted. The same is the exact view of the New Jerusalem later in Revelation. We do not go to Heaven; Heaven comes down to us. The mystic sees the Incarnation at eye level.

Oecumenius sees the first verse of this chapter as the moment of the Incarnation. "The closing and sealing of the scroll signifies the fearful alienation of those inscribed in it and the closing of their mouths from making any plea for justice before God. Therefore, the gradual opening of the seals reveals the gradual recovery of our free and open relationship with God, which the Only Begotten acquired for us when by his own righteousness he set aright our offenses. It is

---

3. Hammond, *Liturgies: Eastern and Western*, 141.

then to be noted that the loosing of each seal reveals a work done by the Lord for our salvation and affected by him against our spiritual enemies . . . Therefore, the first good work of Christ our Savior toward our race, which loosed the first seal of the scroll, is the physical birth of the Lord."[4] Thus, it is by the birth of Christ and the gospel as a whole the seals are broken.

The First Prayer: Revelation 6:1–8

Behold the Lamb
Slain and Broken
Breaks the first of the seven seals.
Hear the thunder of the four living creatures,
"Come!"

You were in Eden, the garden of God.
You are clothed with gold and precious stones.
These were yours from your creation

Look up and see a white horse
Its rider carries a bow
A crown is placed on his head

God set you as the mightiest angel.
You could see God on his throne.
You were righteous
And then you were not
You stole by violence
Your power became sin

Behold the white horse as he rides
He wins many battles
His is the triumph
His is the conquest

You are banished from the mountain of God.
You are ejected, O mighty guardian
Your beauty became your pride

4. Oecumenius, "Oecumenius," 28.

**Your wisdom brought you here
You are thrown to the ground
You are unprotected
Your friends tremble at your fate.
You end is here and you are no more.**[5]

See the second seal
Broken by the Slain Lamb,
Hear the second thundering, "Come!"
We behold the red horse.
It has a mighty sword
It takes peace from the earth
Everywhere is war and murder

**Let us remember Cain who said to his brother,
"Let's go out into the fields."
There Cain killed his brother
There Cain's pride murdered his brother
There Cain's wisdom slaughtered his brother
There peace ended and we are led here**[6]

See the Third Seal break
Hear the sound of "Come!"
Look up and see a black horse
The weapons are scales of famine
Taste starvation
Feel Death
Waste nothing

**The Lord warns us,
"The time is coming
I will send a famine on the land
You will starve for my word
From sea to sea we wander
From border to border we search for the word of the Lord
But it is not found**[7]

5. Ezekiel 28:13–19.
6. Genesis 4:8.
7. Amos 8:11–12.

The Presentation of the Gospel, Part II

I tremble
Behold the Lamb breaks the fourth seal
I tremble
I hear the forth command to arise
I fear

Yea,
**Though I walk through the valley of the shadow of death,
I will fear no evil:
For thou art with me;
Thy rod and thy staff they comfort me**[8]

Look up and see the pale horse.
It is Death,
The Grave is his companion.
They have authority to kill
By sword
By disease
By famine
Let nature turn against us
Death is here.

**We were warned of Death
We see the tree standing in Eden
We are to watch it and mend it
But not to touch it
If we eat it, we will die
We feast upon it daily**[9]

Behold Death and the Grave!

**Adam has brought sin to us all
But what of God's Grace
Adam has brought sin to us all
But God has given Grace through Jesus Christ.**[10]
**Adam's sin—God's Grace
Jesus Christ**

8. Psalm 23:4.
9. Genesis 2:15–17.
10. Romans 5:15.

Behold the Grave riding with Death

Christ reigns until he humbles all enemies
At his feet they will be
Behold death—the last enemy destroyed.[11]

Behold the Death comes to all

Our bodies of death
Transformed into bodies of Life
Scripture fulfilled
"Death is swallowed up in victory."

Behold conquest, war, plague, and death
Let us tremble at the power of our God

Death will have no victory
Death has no sting
The Law gives Sin the Power to Death
But Jesus Christ has brought the victory[12]

Hear the roar of silence
Behold the fifth seal,
See under the altar the souls of all martyred
Remember their faithful testimony.

At God's right hand
Sits Christ in victory
Our sights are these realities of heaven
Since we are raised to a new life in Christ

The witnesses of Israel shout to the Lord
O Sovereign Lord!
Holy One, will you judge the people who belong to this world?
Will you avenge our blood by their blood?

Let us think about the things of heaven
Let us turn from the things of earth.

11. 1 Corinthians 15:25–26.
12. 1 Corinthians 15:54–57.

The Presentation of the Gospel, Part II

See the Lord cloth the witnesses with a white robe
God gives them rest a little longer
For more witnesses will soon join them
Witnesses of Christ will join them under the alter

Remember Judah the Hammer
Taking up a collection to Jerusalem for a sin offering.
In his honor he accounts for the resurrection.
Judah expected the witnesses of Israel to rise again
These things of earth provided for atonement
To deliver from sin[13]
Christ from Heaven has died for us
Our life is hidden in him[14]

The earth trembles,
The monsters of the deep quake
Behold the Lamb stands
The sixth seal torn in his hands

Behold the sixth seal, broken
The curtain in the Temple torn in twain
The sun mourns
The earth shakes
The moon dies red
The tombs are open
The bodies of the saints lay before all
They follow Jesus into Jerusalem
The soldier of mighty Rome
Crowns Jesus the Son of God[15]

Behold the stars falling to the earth
Like green figs falling from a tree shaken by a strong wind they fall
The sky recoils like a wounded scroll
The mountain of the Lord and the isles of the Gentiles
Flew their places

---

13. 2 Maccabees 12:43–45.
14. Colossians 3:1–3.
15. Matthew 27:51–54, cf. Joel 2:31–32.

> **The heavens above melt away**
> **They disappear like a rolled-up scroll**
> **The stars fall from the sky like withered leaves**[16]
>
> Why do you hide yourself among the rocks?
> The kings of the earth,
> The rulers, the generals, the wealthy,
> The powerful,
> Every person is in hiding
> Behold the one sitting on throne
> Behold the wrath of the Lamb has come!
>
> **From Aven, the place of Israel's sin, cries go out.**
> **Thorns and thistles grow on unused altars.**
> **They hide in the**
> **"Bury us!" they cry!**
> **"Fall on us!"**[17]
> **Let us surrender to God's king,**
> **Do not become angry with us, O Lord, for our sins**
> **Do not destroy us in the midst of our injustices**
> **Let us take shelter in him with delight!**[18]
>
> **Amen**

Salvation's History, Heaven's View

In this chapter, we are called to witness from the midpoint between Heaven and earth the view of the Incarnation. With the horsemen, however, we are called to examine ourselves. Perhaps they do represent the evils of John's age, but are we all that different today? Are we not threatened with social collapse, war, and death? This is not a temporal thing, but the human condition brought upon this earth by our sin.

We may see the horses, represented as they are by past pestilences, as the ongoing war, death, and famine mixed with false

---

16. Isaiah 34:4.
17. Hosea 10:8.
18. Psalm 2:12.

religion. This is valid, but it does not serve us well. It does not, as prayer is meant to do, cause us to consider inwardly those things we manifest outwardly. Instead, we must turn inward and see these horses as thin places where our perfection rests. So then, the first horse may in fact be Jesus, or as Victorinus of Petovium says, the Holy Spirit.[19] Oecumenius would see it as the gospel. Both are sent forth by Christ through the Father and both are for the perfecting of God's people. These are valid and needful to consider as we pray, but let us also ponder something else.

Let us not start with Christ, but the human condition. If we were to take this horse and instead of allowing it may be representative of some form of the Christian belief, let us start with the need for the belief. In the Garden, was it not our own intuition we relied upon when we disobeyed God? Throughout the history of Israel, notably when they sought a king, was it not their own power they sought to rely upon? When we first seek to be god, is this not the first moment of our fall? Replace the image of Jesus here with the traditional view of an antichrist rider who seeks to claim for himself that which rightly belongs to Jesus only. We can only seek repair for ourselves if we first know how we are hurt in the first place.

If we see the white horse not as Jesus but as ourselves who regularly attempt to usurp the crown of Christ, we can then properly apply the equine imagery. The red stallion is the devil or some other evil.[20] We have brought this plague upon the earth. Thus the devil brings sin, the black horse, because there is a famine of the word of God upon the earth (Amos 8:11).[21] The pale pony becomes for us the war we wage against God and at one time, against the people of God. Because we are void of God as sinners, we by nature wage war against

---

19. Victorinus of Petovium, *Commentary on the Apocalypse*, 6.1.

20. See the commentaries by Primasius, Tyconius, Caesarius of Arles, Oecumenius, and Andrew of Caesarea.

21. Do not think this refers only to Scripture, but to the command of God and to the order he would have us follow. Early church writers, Oecumenius and Andrew of Caesarea among them, could see in the black horse both sin and false religion. Sin is itself a false religion because we have replaced the order of God with our own chaos.

him and his intended order. It is not like we will win or even know we are in a fight, but the Church testifies that our nature is scarred and thus is prone to rebel.

What is left, then, but to acknowledge all of those we have through our nature murdered because they have stood for God's ordering? This is the scene of the altar. The saints are there, waiting not for our redemption, but for the final elimination of those who oppose the covenant of God. They call for vengeance upon us with every right to do so! We see this played out in the Gospels and Paul's letters where the early believers of Jesus were amazed the Gentiles could likewise be saved. It is not God's plan to destroy us all, but to bring salvation to us all through the redemptive act of Jesus. "The vision clearly depicts for us the signs that occurred at the time of the crucifixion: the earthquake and the turmoil of the earth, the darkness of the sun and the transformation of the full moon into blood."[22] Thus, 6:12–7 is God's answer to the sins represented by the Four Horsemen! "And so, he who boasted that he would put his throne upon the clouds and make himself like unto the Most High, as Isaiah dramatically depicted it, departs with shame and now for the first time learns of his own weakness."[23]

Sin is gone. The balm is given. Our rebellion has ceased by the sacrifice of the one good man. "The third mercy of Christ toward us opened the third seal and restored us, who had been condemned, to God the Father."[24] Those under the altar are now avenged, glorified, and justified because through us they are made perfect.

> The world was not worthy of them. They were refugees in deserts and on the mountains, hiding in caves and holes in the ground. All these won God's approval because of their faith; and yet they did not receive what was promised, because, with us in mind, God had made a better plan, that only with us should they reach perfection. (Hebrews 11:39–40)

22. Oecumenius, "Oecumenius," 32.
23. Oecumenius, "Oecumenius," 29.
24. Oecumenius, "Oecumenius," 29.

The Presentation of the Gospel, Part II

In this chapter the gospel is not just made present, but reasoned out to show us why we need the death, burial, and resurrection of Jesus Christ. Accordingly, in our prayers and liturgical services we must pay specific attention to remember to always focus on the cross in our meditations and preaching. Without it, all hope is vain and we are left still with the plagues we bring about because of our unredeemed humanity.

The Prayer of Contrition, or Deprecation

Oh My Jesus, for us you have been born
Because of our sin, you had to die.
Because or our rebellion, you had to come

We repent of our sins
We have replaced you with our own thought
We have ignored the reason of the Father
We have sought to have others follow us instead of you

We repent of our sins
We repent of calling to the devil for help
We repent of trusting in our flesh for aid
We repent of giving a place to evil in our world

We repent of our sins, O God
We repent of our rebellion against heaven
We repent of the drought we have caused upon the earth
We repent of standing in God's way

We repent of our sins
We repent of the death we have caused
We repent of the wars we wage
We repent of our atheism masked as Christianity

O God judge us not as the altar of souls demand
Give us Nineveh's chance
Tell the prophet to set in the shade of the tree
Take not our part out of your redemptive place, Great King

We are able to repent of sins only because of the cross
Lord, you have saved us from the earthquakes,
From the bloody moons and the falling stars, we are saved
We are saved from the wrath of God and the Lamb
Only because the Cross has caused those things in heaven
We repent because we are saved.

6

The Triumphal Hymn

> Thus prophetically we sing the triumphal hymns for the Church:
> *Rejoice exceedingly, O daughter of Sion,*
> *sing forth, O daughter of Jerusalem . . .*[1]

The triumphal hymn in the liturgy of the Church is quite ancient. St. Ephrem is not the progenitor but the interpreter. "The exclusion of unbelievers, the Triumphal Hymn, Intercession for the Living and Dead, the Invocation of the Holy Spirit, and the rite of Consignation, are distinctly mentioned by S. Ephrem (Syrus) of Edessa, who died a.d. 378."[2] Simply, it is the hymn often sung with Isaiah 6 and Psalm 118 in mind, closing the Preface in the ancient liturgies. It contains "only a general acknowledgment of the duty of thanksgiving, while special passages were inserted according to the day or season, mentioning the particular grounds appropriate to the same."[3]

What makes this chapter a Triumphal Hymn? John is using everything in his arsenal to craft the image of the Lord of Hosts (the prime object of the Triumphal Hymn) recruiting his army. The call

---

1. Denzinger, et. al, *The Sources of Catholic Dogma*, 122.
2. Hammond, *Liturgies: Eastern and Western*, lx.
3. Hammond, *Liturgies: Eastern and Western*, 384.

to assemble is not limited to the tribes of Israel but now the emblem of Christ is bestowed to our entire race. This universality of the cross of Christ is foremost in John's mind as he writes Revelation. As we have just seen, the cross is the center of salvation history. How is the crucified bandit a triumph? "The death on the cross can be called a judgment of sin only because by God's marvelous intervention it was turned into a triumph of God over the apparently triumphant power of sin."[4]

The Apostle Paul tells us death is the final enemy (1 Corinthians 15:26–8). The emblem of Christ is not the sign of death—we must not mistake the cross as such—but is instead the sign of the resurrection. "Death, which, by its very nature, is the end, the destruction of every communication, is changed by him into an act of self-communication; and this is man's redemption, for it signifies the triumph of love over death."[5] The cross is in center view in this chapter.

Revelation 7:1–17

On the four corners of the earth,
Stand the four angels
They have the power to destroy the land and the sea
The four winds are held back
Another angel we see in the east
This angel carries the seal of the living God.
From east to west the angel shouts,
Wait to do your destruction until the seals are given

We walk with the angels
Through the streets of Jerusalem we walk
The angel puts a mark on the foreheads of the repentant.
We cry,
O God! Save Jerusalem if you find but ten righteous souls!
We weep with the angel who says

---

4. Weiss, *Christ, The Beginnings of Dogma*, 109.
5. Ratzinger, *Behold The Pierced One: An Approach to a Spiritual Christology*, 25.

The Triumphal Hymn

"The sins of the people are too great to be spared.
Our land is full of murder
The city is broken and unjust.
Our God is mocked
So he has no pity
He will not spare but repay[6]

Hear God assembling his army
144,000 sealed from all Israel
From Judah, from Reuben, from Gad
Asher, Naphtali, and Manasseh give 12,000
Simeon 12,000 and Levi 12,000 and Issachar 12,000
Zebulon, Joseph, and Benjamin and their 12,000
Only Dan deserts our cause

We hear the Lord promise,
He will send out his angels as a trumpet
They will gather his chosen ones
From the ends of the earth
From the ends of heaven he gathers them[7]

We see an immense crowd
We cannot count them all!
Babel's tower repents by this crowd
They stand before the throne
They stand before the Lamb.
They are clothed in white robes
Palm branches are given to them.

The Day of the Son of David
And his emblem of salvation is here
The nations will unite to him
This is the day the Lord will reach out his hand
With the fires of Pentecost, his hand will reach out
His ensign rises to call the exiles home
He from the ends of the earth, Judah and Israel is called home.[8]

6. Ezekiel 9:4, 8–10.
7. Matthew 24:31.
8. Isaiah 11:10–12.

Shout with the remnant!
They shout with a mighty shout,
"Salvation is of our God
Salvation comes from the one who sits on the throne
Salvation comes from the Lamb!"

When the little horn has torn apart the saints
Remember that near Jerusalem a horseman appeared
He was clothed in white with weapons of gold.
All praised the merciful God
In the midst of defeat their heart was strengthened
Heaven was their ally
The Lord had mercy on them.[9]
Victory was theirs
Praise God with palm branches
Praise God with harps, cymbals and stringed instruments
Sing to him hymns and songs
God has won the battle[10]

All the angels stand around the throne.
Before the throne they fall with their faces to the ground to worship God
They sing,
"Amen! Blessing and glory
Wisdom and thanksgiving
Honor and power
And Strength belong to our God forever and ever!"

Carry ivy-wreathed rods
Bring beautiful branches
Bring the fronds of palm
Offer hymns of thanksgiving to him
He has made holy his sanctuary.[11]

"Who are these clothed in white?
Where did they come from?

---

9. 2 Maccabees 11:8–10.
10. 1 Maccabees 13:51.
11. 2 Maccabees 10:7.

The Triumphal Hymn

These are the ones who died as witnesses.
They are washed the blood of the Lamb
His blood has made their robes white."

Since the time of the prophets
Since the time of the apostles
Since the time of the fathers
Since the time of the reformers
Since our own time
There has never been such great a distress[12]
We panic at every rumor of war
We are frightened by gossip
Natural occurrences become horrors
The course of sin scares us
Our ancestors were arrested, persecuted, and killed,
But we fear the slightest embrace of silence
Fearful we no longer rule
Fearful our color is dimming
They were hated
We are treated fairly
We complain
They met their fate as directed by God
We do not endure because we are weak
Scared of our own shadow[13]

Their obedience is why they stand in front of God's throne
This is why they serve him day and night in his Temple
The one who sits on the throne will give them shelter
They will never again be hungry or thirsty
They will never be scorched by the heat of the sun
The Lamb sits on the throne as their shepherd.
He leads them to springs of eternal water
God wipes the tears from their eyes.

Will we have a share in the everlasting covenant?
God has given what he promised

12. 1 Maccabees 9:27.
13. Matthew 24:6–13.

Praying in God's Theater

> He has put his Temple among them forever.
> He makes his home among them.
> He is their God, and they are his people.
> The nations know he is God
> He makes Israel holy.[14]

> Amen

Victory

> If therefore, at the present time, having the earnest, we do cry, "Abba, Father," what shall it be when, on rising again, we behold Him face to face; when all the members shall burst out into a continuous hymn of triumph, glorifying Him who raised them from the dead, and gave the gift of eternal life? For if the earnest, gathering man into itself, does even now cause him to cry, "Abba, Father," what shall the complete grace of the Spirit effect, which shall be given to men by God? It will render us like unto Him, and accomplish the will of the Father; for it shall make man after the image and likeness of God.[15]

"Then carrying palms, the tokens of victory, with flaming tapers, with sounding hymns, and with fragrant incense, celebrating the triumph of his heavenly victory, they laid down the sacred relics, and buried them in the cemetery which had been long ago constructed by him, where too from henceforth, and even to this day, miraculous virtues cease not to show themselves."[16] This is the scene recorded of the last martyr of Alexandria, a Bishop named Peter. We must note the similarities between this scene and the scene in John's volume. Victory is declared by the ancient symbol of the palm leaf. It is possible the ancient celebrants followed well this path laid down by our writer.

14. Ezekiel 37:26–28.
15. St. Irenaeus, *Against Heresies*, 5.8.1 in *ANF*, 1:533.
16. "The Genuine Acts of Peter" in *ANF*, 6:268.

The Triumphal Hymn

When Judas Maccabee won against the Greeks, liberating God's Holy City, they celebrated by using palm branches. When Rome captured the land of Israel, they minted coins showing the broken palm branch. No doubt, these coins were in John's mind, if not in his possession, as he crafted this passage.

Imagine, for a moment, John setting his coin before him. Behold the symbol of Roman occupation. It was not just the coin, but everything placed on the coin. In John's spiritual vision, he sees the healed palm branches and the ultimate triumph of God over the plagues of this life. This is why Jesus was greeted with the palm branch because he was the victory of God. This is why St. Peter of Alexandria was buried with palm branches because he experienced the victory of God. Here, in John's heaven, a great number of people innumerable stand assembled by God in the ultimate triumph because of the victory of God.

No doubt, because this scene follows so closely to John's reimaging of the crucifixion we should look towards a better interpretation of this passage, that this is the resurrection. When we pray as the Church Militant we likewise pray with the whole communion of Saints including the Church Triumphant. When we stand in our liturgical celebrations or kneel in our moments of prayer, we are not doing this alone or only in in a single place in time, but we do so as the Church, the body of Christ spread out across time, space, earth, and heaven. This is the power of prayer, to connect us through the cross (Revelation 6.12–17) to the great multitude in heaven. It is through the cross we are given victory (7.10) and find the power (7.12) to progress.

The scene in heaven is not a future event, but if we take seriously the words of the angel (7.13), then this scene is taking place this very moment just out of reach of our human eyes. Our loved ones, our fathers and mothers in the faith and all of those now unseen along with the Prophets and the Apostles are taking part in God's great Triumphal Entrance *now*.

Praying in God's Theater

It would be impossible for the original audience not to have heard this passage next to the several from the Old Testament. If we compare this passage to Ezekiel 34, we find the story of two shepherds (Revelation 7:17). One shepherd falsely leads people, giving them only a muted spiritual experience. The True Shepherd, Christ, is the one who leads us to the living presence.[17] In listening to Ezekiel, we can hear the Eucharistic celebration in John rather clearly. It is not difficult to see; rather, it is severely impossible to miss the Eucharistic celebratory language in his passage. In this passage, we see the whole tribe of the human race united by the sacraments of baptism (the robes) and the Eucharist (the blood; the lack of hunger and thirst).

A Prayer of Thanksgiving

> We pray to you, O God,
> Give us peace.
> Hold back the angels of your wrath
> Seal us as your servants forever.
>
> Gather together your ancient people
> From the four corners of the earth
> Bring home the exiled
> Restore your people called Israel
>
> Forget not us, O Lord, we Gentiles
> We stand before you scattered
> We have caused everything to separate us
> But, unite us as one and let us proclaim to you the victory
> Give us the hammer's palm branches
>
> We sing of salvation
> We glory you, O God, and your Lamb
> Blessing, glory, wisdom
> Thanksgiving, honor, power, and might
> To you, O God, forever and ever.

17. Barber, *Coming Soon*, 114.

The Triumphal Hymn

O My Jesus,
By your blood, you have brought us into your people
You have rescued us from the tribulation of sin
We have washed our robes in your blood

O God, we will serve you always
Because of you, we no longer hunger and thirst
We no longer suffer exhaustion
You like a shepherd have leaded us to the springs of eternal life

7

The Prayers of the Faithful

"After the sermon the catechumens are dismissed;
the faithful will remain."[1]

We have just seen the gospel presented from the point of view of heaven and earth, resting in what the Celtic Christians have called the thin places.[2] "The Gospel is to be read before the oblation, or before the dismissal of the catechumens, or after the Epistle, so that not only the faithful, but also the catechumens, penitents, and all others may hear the word of God and the sermon of the bishop. For it is well known that through the hearing of preaching many have been led to the faith."[3] If we follow something of the structure of the ancient liturgy, we would now arrive at the point of the dismissal of the catechumens, the uninitiated believers who, while they believe in Christ, do not yet know the mysteries of the Faith. Their role in the liturgy thus far is a sign of the thin place. They can see the drama of the liturgy, but only in a small part.

---

1. Augustine, *Sermo 237*, as found in O'Brien, *A History of the Mass*, 248.
2. For a general introduction to Celtic Christianity, see Balzer, *Thin Places: An Evangelical Journey into Celtic Christianity*.
3. Hefele, *A History of the Councils of the Church, Volume 4*, 137.

Several ancient Syrian liturgies (c. 350) had the catechumens and others unable, or unworthy, to receive the Eucharist dismissed with silent prayers. "Let none of the catechumens, no men of little faith, none of the penitents, nor of the unclean draw near to this divine mystery."[4] Likewise, the silence is meant to precede the Prayers of the Faithful (this chapter) and the Great Entrance (see below).

We know better what our faith entails. We have just seen from the heavenly realm the gospel performed. We know more about the doctrines of grace. Now, as we prepare ourselves for prayer, having moved past the imperfections of an immature faith, we must notice the silence. It may do the supplicant well to take such a space as described herein to collect their thoughts, to pause for a moment and clear their mind. Let the stray thoughts be considered the unworthy attendants to the table, our vanity the unlearned believer who must be removed before the instructions to the mystery begin.

Revelation 8:1–13

With the Angels, stand silent
Behold the Lamb slain
The Seal Seventh broken
All of heaven is silence
But we do not confuse silence with peace

Stand in silence the prophet commands,
In his presence quiet
The day of the Lord is here
We are prepared for slaughter
Our executioners chosen[5]
Let the world return
Then shall the world return to chaotic silence
Silence before God said let there be
Let a new time shout from this silence
Let a new age arise

4. Hammond, *Liturgies: Eastern and Western*, 149.
5. Zephaniah 1:7.

Let corruption perish
Let the earth restore the sleeping
Let the dust gather our remains and give us life
Let the sea give up her dead[6]

Look and see the seven angels
They stand before God
He gives them seven trumpets

O Lord God, Great and Eternal King!
Send, O Lord,
Your Archangel Michael to help us
To deliver us from all enemies, visible and invisible
O Archangel Michael, angel of the Lord and vanquisher of demons!
Suppress all opponents
Make them meek as sheep
Disperse them like dust before the wind.[7]

See an angel with a gold incense censer
Before the altar the angel stands.
In his hands is a great amount of incense
Mix, angel, mix the incense with our prayers
O angel, give this as your offering to God

Let my supplication rise before you like incense,
Let my hands be like an evening offering.[8]

Watch the smoke of the incense, mixed with prayers,
The angel pours them out on the alter
The prayers ascend to God
Watch now the angel fill the censer with fire from the altar
Upon the earth it rains down
Thunder crashes, lightning flashes, the earth quakes.
The seven trumpets are ready to blow.

The cherubim stand at the south end of the Temple
The cloud of glory fills the inner courtyard

6. 4 Esdras 7:30–32.
7. I have modified the prayer of St. Michael.
8. Psalm 141:2.

The glory of the LORD rises up above the cherubim
The Temple fills with this cloud of glory
Hear the voice of God Almighty in the wings of the cherubim[9]

Shout at the first blast of the trumpet!
Hail and fire mixed with blood rain upon the earth.
Behold as the Garden of God lay wasted, to a third of all we see.

We one said
"We shall never be shaken"
We are complacent
Injustice does not upset us
"We shall not be moved."[10]

Mourn the blast of the second trumpet
See the great mountain of fire thrown into the sea.
The water in the sea becomes blood
All life in the sea becomes death, to a third

A third of your people die from disease and famine.
A third slaughtered by the enemy outside
A third scattered to the winds chased by sword.
Only then will the anger of the Lord relent.
But in God's anger there is knowledge
In God's anger, all will know repentance[11]

O Lord our God,
We cried to you for help
You restore our health.[12]
His anger lasts a moment,
His favor lasts a lifetime!
We weep in the night
In the morning we are met with joy.[13]

---

9. Ezekiel 10.3–5.
10. Psalm 30.7.
11. Ezekiel 5.12–14.
12. Psalm 30.2.
13. Psalm 30.5.

Praying in God's Theater

The third angel blows his trumpet
A great star falls from the sky
It falls on a third of the rivers
On the springs of water it falls.
It is wormwood, bitterness, to a third it makes the water bitter
To a third, it kills

We tremble when God says,
"Look! I will feed them with wormwood
They will drink poison."[14]
He has fills us with bitterness
We drink the bitter cup of sorrow[15]

We are frightened, but we must hear the fourth angel
The trumpet blows and darkness covers the cosmos to a third.
We have day and night and perpetual dusk

His anger lasts a moment,
His favor lasts a lifetime!
We weep in the night
In the morning we are met with joy.[16]

An eagle cries loudly in the air,
"Fear, horror, and dread to all who belong to this world
Panic, dismay, and terror will be heard in the final three trumpets."

We are in the day of the death of sun at noon
The earth lays dark in the day
Our rituals of celebration are songs of mourning
We weep where we should praise
We grieve, but it is not our son who has died
Behold the bitterness of wormwood[17]
His anger lasts a moment,
His favor lasts a lifetime!
We weep in the night

14. Jeremiah 9:15.
15. Lamentations 3:15.
16. Psalm 30:5.
17. Amos 8:9–10.

> In the morning we are met with joy.[18]
> God turns our mourning into celebration.
> The Lord clothes us with joy
> Our praises replace the silence.
> O Lord our God, we will give you thanks forever![19]
>
> Amen

The Prayers of the Faithful

The catechumens and the unworthy are removed. Then a prayer led by the qualified begins. The mystery is unfolded for the initiated as they pray. It is no longer a fearsome destruction of the world the Christian sees, but the "Confession of Faith, Fraction, Consignation, and Commixture."[20] It is worth noting the development of the four degrees of penance in the early church, mirroring both the four steps of the Eucharist and the four trumpets of Revelation 8.[21]

What might we make of the first trumpet? Like the plagues of Egypt, the fire raining down from heaven is mixed with hail (Exodus 9:23–4). In Psalm 78:47 God is said to have destroyed his people's vineyards with hail. "To the wise man his own life is a vineyard, his own mind is a vineyard, and a vineyard also is his own conscience. For he that is truly wise will allow nothing in himself to remain uncultivated, nothing unprofitable."[22] Thus, this prayer becomes a

---

18. Psalm 30:5.
19. Psalm 30:11–12.
20. Hammond, *Liturgies: Eastern and Western*, xxvii.
21. "By the end of the third century as many as four degrees of penance were appointed, through which offenders had to pass in order to a reconciliation." (Newman, *An Essay on the Development of Christian Doctrine*, 413.) See also Lépicier, *Indulgences, Their Origin, Nature, and Development*, 92–5. Cardinal Lépicier details at length the four degrees, placing this tradition in the "Oriental" (or Eastern) Churches. Earlier, Simkins cited Cyprian (a Bishop of Carthage) as the originator of this tradition. See Simkins, *The Oriental and Grecian Philosophy*, 108–9.
22. Saint Bernard, *St. Bernard's Sermons on the Canticle of Canticles, Volume 2*, 218.

prayer to remove from us those things not worthy of God. As the Nestorian liturgy remembers, "That he remove from us in his grace the sword and captivity and robbery and earthquakes and hail and famine and pestilence and all evil plagues that are against the body."[23] We are called to rid ourselves of those things separating us from God.

The second trumpet and the destruction it brings is a call to awake to the reality of our poverty. St. Ephrem says, "for the abyss did not bring forth the Flood against them that they might take refuge on the heights, but sin drowned [them], while penance brought salvation, that is, righteousness brought deliverance."[24] This trumpet is meant to remind us our wealth (represented by the ships) will not secure us a place in heaven nor is a concern of God's. As God has destroyed our internal vineyards, he will destroy our internal mammon. Think about the Church of Laodicea with its false affluence. To rely on our treasure, then, is to deny to God his place as our helper. He imparts to us righteousness and grace. It is through the prayers of penance we must take these things and properly use them. God will purge the falseness, if we let him.

We have asked God to clear our conscious (first trumpet), to remove our false grace (second trumpet), and now we will ask God to clear our false religion (third trumpet). In Jeremiah 9:15 and 23:15, God promises to give to Israel wormwood, a bitter and foul tasting plant used in some medicines.[25] Why? Israel descended to worshiping in idolatry. An imported false religion removed the proper worship of the Most High.

During the time of John, a Greek herbalist named Aretaeus of Cappadocia recommended mixing wormwood and another particular flora, acacia, to create a working medicine.[26] Acacia was used in building the altar of incense (Exodus 27.1–8; 38.1–7). Wormwood

---

23. Brightman, *Liturgies: Eastern and Western*, 265.

24. Murray, *Symbols of Church and Kingdom: a Study in Early Syriac Tradition*, 219–20.

25. See also Amos 5:7, 6:13 and Deuteronomy 29:18.

26. Aretaeus, *The Extant Works of Aretaeus, The Cappadocian*, 433.

tasted bitter, worked quickly. Acacia was moderately successful but tasted pleasant. It was only when the worst sort of illness remained, like false religion, did wormwood become necessary. Thus, the third trumpet speaks of God's judgment upon our false religious works.

This is not, as some Protestants might supposed, a condemnation on all religious ritual, but on a religious ritual where we are the center of the presentation.

> Alas, in regard to things spiritual, the foolishness of many is this, that they in the secular sense look upon the speaker as an actor, and the listeners as theatergoers who are to pass judgment upon the artist. But the speaker is not the actor—not in the remotest sense. No, the speaker is the prompter. There are no mere theatergoers present, for each listener will be looking into his own heart. The stage is eternity, and the listener, if he is the true listener (and if he is not, he is at fault) stands before God during the talk. The prompter whispers to the actor what he is to say, but the actor's repetition of it is the main concern—is the solemn charm of the art. The speaker whispers the word to the listeners. But the main concern is earnestness: that the listeners by themselves, with themselves, and to themselves, in the silence before God, may speak with the help of this address.
>
> The address is not given for the speaker's sake, in order that men may praise or blame him. The listener's repetition of it is what is aimed at. If the speaker has the responsibility for what he whispers, then the listener has an equally great responsibility not to fall short in his task. In the theater, the play is staged before an audience who are called theatergoers; but at the devotional address, God himself is present. In the most earnest sense, God is the critical theatergoer, who looks on to see how the lines are spoken and how they are listened to: hence here the customary audience is wanting. The speaker is then the prompter, and the listener stands openly before God. The listener, if I may say so, is the actor, who in all truth acts before God.[27]

27. Kierkegaard, *Purity of Heart is To Will One Thing*, 180–1.

If God is not the center of our worship, individual or corporate, then it is false worship. In seeking God's help to restore the right relationship with him is to finally acknowledge God's rightful place.

Finally, we hear the fourth trumpet. "The day earnestly desired, by the prayers of all has come; and after the dreadful and loathsome darkness of a long night, the world has shone forth irradiated by the light of the Lord."[28] What is the nature of this darkness? I can surely see everything, the unworthy says. And yet, those who know the mystery of the faith realize even our brightest days are still darkness if it is not the Day of the Lord. If it is not Christ who brings the light, then all light is false. We who have long been in darkness have seen a great light (Isaiah 9:2).

"Those persons in whom their desires live, and hinder the knowledge of God, God will swallow up in His wrath, either in the next life, in the purifying pains of purgatory, or in this, in afflictions and sufferings, sent to detach them from their desires, or in the mortification of those very desires voluntarily undergone. God doeth this to take away the false light of desire between Himself and us, which dazzles us and hinders us from knowing Him; and that, the intellect becoming clear, the ravage of desire may be repaired."[29] The angel does not say what or who struck the lights in the heavens, but the event is in God's unfolding plan. This is God swallowing up our false darkness, our crafted wisdom, through the penitential prayers.

This reality presented here is either traumatic or a relief. Either we find real freedom as we surrender ourselves to Christian enslavement or we continue arrogantly challenging God. When the catechumens and others unworthy were dismissed, that was our moment to step away, to leave the service unhurried and unchallenged. But we stayed. We who have heard the gospel and knew the consequences stayed nevertheless to participate in the prayers for the faithful. Because of this, we are given either to relief or worry. If the sound of a trumpet gives you fright, still your heart by repairing it to Christ.

28. Cyprian of Carthage, *On the Lapsed*, in *ANF,* 5:437.
29. Saint John of the Cross, *The Ascent of Mount Carmel*, 37.

Take either the acacia now or the wormwood later, but take the medicine of Christ.

A Prayer of Supplication

> O Great God,
> We stand before your altar
> Take our prayers and consider them
> Remove from us the stench of sin
>
> Let us order our lives to you
> Let us see only you ahead of us
> Cleanse our rituals of sin
>
> O Lord, give us wormwood
> We have replaced you in our lives
> We have sinned against you
> Our water is poison and yet we drink
>
> O Lord, give us light
> You have caused the light to be stricken
> It is for our own understanding
> Forgive us, O Lord, our sins

8

The Preparation for the Great Entrance

"Like the smoke of the goodly incense and the savour of the sweet censer receive, O Christ our Saviour, the request and prayer of thy servants."[1]

The ninth chapter of John's liturgical masterpiece is the harbinger of repentance. This is John's drama before God and we must allow him to tell his story. While we would like to see all come easily to repentance (2 Peter 3:9), John reminds this is not the case, at least not yet. Even while the great Eucharistic call is issued, even when the need for repentance is demonstrated by the dismissal of the catechumens, many will stand in the congregation of the Lord unrepentant.

> The spiritual man, therefore, must purify his will, and render it insensible to this empty rejoicing, remembering that beauty, and all other natural graces, are earth, from the earth, and soon return to it; that comeliness and grace are but smoke and vapour; and if he would escape falling into vanity, he must esteem them as such, and direct his heart upwards unto God beyond them all, rejoicing and delighted that God is all beauty and all grace in Himself

---

1. Brightman, *Liturgies: Eastern and Western*, 249.

The Preparation for the Great Entrance

supremely, infinitely above all created things. "They shall perish," saith the Psalmist, "but Thou remainest, and all of them shall grow old like a garment." If, therefore, our rejoicing is not in God, it will always be false and delusive. It is to this that those words of Solomon apply which he addressed to that joy which has its sources in created things: "To mirth, I said, Why art thou vainly deceived?" that is when the heart suffers itself to be attracted by created things.[2]

Revelation 9:1–21

With the fifth angel we see a star fall
This angel has a key to the unending abyss
We tremble when it opens
Smoke pours out, a furnace fit for the King of Babylon
Our view is nothing now by ash

Oh God in Heaven
You are boundless and sovereign
The sinners have idols
Made by our hands, of silver and of gold
Mouths speaking not and eyes blind
Hears useless and noses pointless
Hands made to feel but failing
Carried about because they are lame
Speaking not, but heard
We make our idols and become the same
But O Israel, trust the LORD!
He is our helper and our shield.[3]

Our pain is caused by the infection of the smoke
The locusts plague us like scorpions
They harm not the green creation, only us
We do not have the seal of God

2. Saint John of the Cross, *The Ascent of Mount Carmel*, 302.
3. Psalm 115:3–9.

But we give thanks to the LORD
We proclaim his greatness.
We will tell the whole world know what he has done.
Let us sing to him of his praises
Tell of his wonderful deeds.
His name will exult us
Let us rejoice, we who worship the Lord.
Let us search for the Lord and for his strength;
We will continually pursue him.
We will forget not the wonders he has performed[4]

We are tortured but not killed
Our pain is that of poison.
We mourn as unto death, seeking it
But death is not ours to find
We long for death
But death flees from us

We remember his decrees,
We remember the children of Abraham,
The descendants of Jacob are his chosen ones
They are never forgotten
He is the Lord our God.
Behold his justice flooding the land
Forever God attends his promises[5]

King Abaddon, King Apollyon
The king rises from the unending abyss, his army ready to destroy
His army is fearsome
They are given gold crowns on their human heads
Their hair is like women's and their teeth like a lion
Their armor or iron does not weigh down their wings
They torment us with their poison
Their battle is with us
Behold their King Destroyer

---

4. Psalm 105:1–5.
5. Psalm 105:5–8.

The Preparation for the Great Entrance

Blow the trumpet in Jerusalem!
Call for God's army from his holy mountain!
We tremble because this is the Lord's Day.
The day is dark and mournful
The ash of torment hides the sun
Behold God's army appears!
Should we praise or hide?
Fire goes before them; fire trials them
They march to Eden
But nothing behind them remains except desolation.[6]

We pray for nothing more
One terror has past
We pray for nothing more
Two terrors remain
We pray for peace

We are only a few men in number,
Very few, and strangers here
We wandered from nation to nation,[7]
From kingdom to people we roam
Oppression is not permitted to us
Our God protects us
We are his anointed ones and his prophets,
Our God protects us[8]

The Sixth Angel stands
The Voice stands in the presence of God
The Voices command "Release!"
The four angels waiting release
Death follows
War Follows
Troops of lions, fire, and hell follow
We tremble in fear
Where is our God?

6. Joel 2:1–3.
7. See the Epistle to Diognetus.
8. Psalm 105:12–15.

Praying in God's Theater

The earth shakes,
The heavens quake.
The sun and moon hide,
The stars die.
God leads the column with a shout
A terrible thing is the Day of the Lord, but Great
Who will survive?
The Lord says,
"Repent! There is still time
To me your hearts give
Come with sacrifice"[9]

What do we make of death?
The army massacres by plagues and by hell
They kill by their mouth and by their tail
Their tails are snakes that kill
But those who survive refuse to repent
They still worship idols
They still worship idols who cannot save
They do not repent of their murders
They still yet dwell in their immorality

But God will bring out his people with joy
We will shout with joy
The land of the nations is ours
The fruit of our labors are ours
We will keep His statutes
We will observe His laws,
Praise the Lord![10]
We will trust the LORD!
He is our comforter and our shield.[11]

Amen

---

9. Joel 2:10–12.
10. Psalm 105:43–45.
11. Psalm 115:3–9.

Repentance

If we are given to a conservative historical imagination, we may allow the current Armenian liturgy is somewhat derived from the liturgy St. Gregory brought from Caesarea as the tradition states. As Hammond noted, the Armenian Rite has some characteristics of both the Constantinopolitan (Greek) and Roman (Latin) liturgies. "An inspection of the Liturgy itself bears out this probability; for, though there are some palpable later alterations, both from Constantinopolitan and from Latin sources, the chief characteristics of the Armenian, and the wording of some of the prayers, tally very closely with corresponding parts of S. Basil's Liturgy."[12] If the ancient liturgies of the Church find something of a progenitor in John's *piyyutim*, then we would do no harm in finding for ourselves something of an interpretation of Revelation 9 in an ancient liturgy.

The Armenian liturgy provides for us an applicable elucidation for this current chapter. However, we must not leave John's Jewish context. Just as we can propose a move forward (as in the case of ancient Christian liturgies), we can propose an origin for what is before us. In 9.1-6, John is concerned with the billowing smoke from the abyss. Place your attention on the smoke and not what comes out of the smoke. In John's religious world, smoke had a special connotation. It is the smoke of repentance.

Turning to the Dead Sea Scrolls, we find an image similar to the one we see in Revelation. The ancient author writes, "and they will not save their souls from the mystery of ex[istence. And this will be for you the sign that this is happening. When those born of sin are locked up,] evil will disappear before justice as [darkness] disapp[ears before light. As smoke vanishes, and no longer exists, so will] [ev]il [vanish] for ever."[13] There is more. In 4Q491 8–10, we see the image of a High Priest taking his position, surrounded by other

12. Hammond, *Liturgies: Eastern and Western*, xlix.
13. As found in Martinez and Tigchelaar, *The Dead Sea Scrolls Study Edition*, 663.

priests, to take up one of their holy writings and begin to speak. "Be strong!" the priest will say! He commends to his congregation valor, telling them to not be afraid of the army before them because it is the wicked congregation. Soon their power will disappear with the smoke and only the righteous will survive! The smoke is very much a part of the ancient liturgy at Qumran.[14]

It is also a part of the liturgy of the Jacobite Syrian Christian Church, traditionally founded by the Apostle Thomas during his tenure in India.[15] During a portion of the service wherein the priest mixes the chalice while preparing for penitence, the prayer of the congregation reads in part, "*From everlasting*—Let the voice of our ministry be a key that openeth the gates of heaven and may the archangels say from out their ranks How sweet is the voice of the earth-born! The Lord quickly answer their request! May we be pardoned and cleansed and sanctified and purified and purged from all the filth of sin by this smoke of odours which we offer before thee now, o our Lord and our God, and at all times for ever. I have sinned against thee, o thou that hast pity on a sinner: receive my supplication and forgive me my faults: o Lord the lord of all, have mercy on me."[16]

Now, let us return back to the ancient Armenian liturgy. What follows is a part of the liturgy falling before the Great Entrance, called of *The Preparation of the Ministers*:

> Then the priest coming into the middle of the church washes his hands saying
>
> *Ktzord* I will wash my hands in innocency, O Lord: and so will I Go to thine altar
>
> *Phokh* Be thou my judge, O Lord, for I have walked innocently

---

14. See also, Chazon, et al., *Liturgical Perspectives: Prayer and Poetry in Light of the Dead Sea Scrolls*.

15. It is based in Kerala, India. The liturgy has close affinities to other Antiochian liturgies.

16. Brightman, *Liturgies: Eastern and Western*, 71–2.

The Preparation for the Great Entrance

(Congregation reads) *and the rest of Psalm 26*

Glory be to the Father and to the Son and to the Holy Ghost

Now and ever world without end. Amen.

The priest

And for the sake of the holy mother of God, O Lord, accept our supplications and save us

The deacon

Let us make the holy mother of God and all the saints our intercessors with the Father in heaven

that he be pleased to have mercy and in his pity to save his creatures

Almighty Lord our God, save and have mercy

The priest

Receive, O Lord, our supplications through the intercession of the holy mother of God, the immaculate mother of thine only begotten Son, and through the supplications of all thy saints. Hear us, O Lord, and have mercy: pardon expiate and forgive us our sins and account us worthy with praises to glorify thee with thy Son and the Holy Ghost now and ever and world without end. Amen.

Then turning towards the people he says

I confess before God and the holy mother of God and before all the saints and before you, fathers and brethren, all the sins I have committed: for I have sinned in thought word and deed and with every sin committed of men: I have sinned, I have sinned: I pray you request for me of God forgiveness

The [priests] standing by answer

God the potentate have mercy on thee and grant thee forgiveness of all thy trespasses past and present, deliver thee from those in the time to come, confirm thee in every good work and give thee rest in the life to come. Amen

The priest answers

God the lover of men set you also free and forgive you all your trespasses, give you time for repentance and for the practice of good works and direct also your life in time to come: through the grace of the Holy Ghost the potentate and merciful unto whom be glory for ever. Amen.

The bystanders

Remember us before the immortal lamb of God

The priest

Ye shall be remembered before the immortal lamb of God.

The clerks then say Ps. 100 in antiphon

O be joyful in the Lord all ye lands Glory be. Now and ever.

The deacon

Through the holy church let us beseech the Lord that through her he will deliver us from sins and save us through the grace of his mercy

Almighty Lord our God, save and have mercy

The priest

In the midst of this temple and in the presence of these divine and bright holy signs and holy place, bowing down in fear we worship, we glorify thine holy marvelous and triumphant {Resurrection} and unto thee with the Father and the Holy Ghost we offer blessing and glory now and ever and world without end. Amen

The Preparation for the Great Entrance

The priest saying Ps. 43 in antiphon with the deacon goes up to the altar

Ktzord I will go unto the altar of god even unto the God of my joy and gladness

The deacon

Phokh Give sentence with me, o God, and defend my cause against the ungodly people

and the rest of Ps. 43

Glory be. Now and ever.[17]

The Anaphora of Saints Addai and Mari belongs to the Liturgy of the Nestorians and is thought to be among the oldest, perhaps third century Edessa, beginning life as an Eucharistic hymn.[18] It begins with the preparation of the loaves, where the priest (unlike other liturgies) actually prepares the loaves from scratch. Might we see something of the preparation of the Eucharist here? It is not merely the repentance of sins we see, but in view is the oven used to bake the bread.

What should we learn and apply to our prayers from these ancient liturgies? Throughout these various ancient and multicultural sources we find a common element. We must repent. In this chapter John stresses the refusal of the people to repent along with God's patience. When the torment proceeding from the smoke is released, the divine command limits the destruction of the earth only to those who refuse to repent. While they are tormented they are not allowed to die.

Is this the sign of a psychopathic God? Perhaps God simply desires to torment his creation for as long as possible.

---

17. Brightman, *Liturgies: Eastern and Western*, 415–16.

18. Macomber, *The Oldest Known Text of the Anaphora of the Apostles Addai and Mari*, 335–36. Saint Addai is said to be a disciple of Thomas the Apostle, and Mari a disciple of Addai. Like other Orthodox Churches, it provides a continuous lineage back to the Twelve.

Praying in God's Theater

On the other hand, we must look at it through the lens of grace. As the author of 2 Peter says, God desires all should come to repentance and therefore delays his judgment. While praying, we must not forget the delay we see and the questions it raises regarding why evil seems to reign while the righteous suffer are but questions based in *our* worldview. John is telling us to maintain our purgative preparation. Yes, God calls to them, begging them to repent before judgment. He billows smoke to cleanse them. He stands before the altar waiting to measure out the body and the blood of Jesus for healing. The delay in punishing evil is the ultimate sign of God's grace.

A Prayer of Contrition

Great God, send from heaven your angel
Let a star that falls, your angel brings us your word
Purify us with the smoke from your nostrils, O Lord

O My Jesus, save us from our sins
Temper your wrath until all repent
Lock up those born of sin
Let their evil disappear
Bring forth your justice
Let us be purged of our iniquities.

O God, destroy our sins but save us
Say unto Apollyon, 'Not Yet.'
Give us time, O Lord.

We repent of the words of hands that have placed you
We repent of our worship of false gods, of demons
We repent of our worship of gold and silver
We repent of worshiping those things that are not you

We repent of our sins against you
We repent of our sins against each other
We repent of stealing from you your worship, O Lord.

Destroy our sins, but save us.

9

The Cherubic Hymn

> "I have sinned against Heaven, and before Thee, and am unworthy to come into the presence of this Thy holy and spiritual table.[1]

We are moving closer to the Eucharist, to the certain unity with God, and to the return of Jesus. We must remember the premise that our prayer and our Eucharistic celebrations are not merely a temporal thing. No, instead we must remind ourselves both prayer and the Eucharistic are doors to Heaven. Hence, when John sees the angel coming to him, he writes in such a way as to reposition himself on earth, the place he left in chapter 4, because John is in the thin place, the open door to Heaven.

> The corporeal visions are visions of all material things in heaven and earth, visible to the soul in a certain light emanating from God, in which the distant things of heaven and earth may be seen. The other visions of incorporeal things require a higher light: thus visions of incorporeal substances, as of angels and of souls, are neither frequent nor natural in this life; and still less so is the vision of the divine essence, which is peculiar to the blessed, unless it be communicated transiently by a dispensation of God, or

---

1. *The Divine Liturgy of St. James* in *ANF,* 7:537.

by conservation of our natural life and condition, and the abstraction of the spirit.[2]

St. John of the Cross is not speaking out of the ordinary, but taking the total of Christian revelatory experience and giving it a revelatory construct. Our original author is experiencing such a vision whereby he sees angels and souls. He is suspended between heaven and earth, in that unique place where only a few have trod. What he sees is an angel who some commenters have said to be Jesus but is more likely Michael or one of the other archangels, perhaps Gabriel. What does this angel do? He brings to John more verse and more images.

Revelation 10:1–11

We pray as we see from heaven come another angel,
A cloud surrounds him
A rainbow crowns his head.
His face shines like the sun,
His feet are pillars of fire.

Behold the one from the Sea
The one who went ahead of Israel
Guide us O Lord in the day by the cloud
In the night surround us by fire
We will travel day and night
Do not remove from us your angel[3]
With Daniel we see the son of man in the clouds of heaven
He stands in the presence of the Holy One
He is given sovereignty over the nations,
Let Babel's Curse turn
God's rule is eternal and his kingdom forever[4]

---

2. Saint John of the Cross, *The Ascent of Mount Carmel*, 198.
3. Exodus 13:21.
4. Daniel 7:13–14.

The Cherubic Hymn

In his hand was a small scroll opened
On the sea he stands and on the land
He roars with the shout of a lion

O Lord, do not do anything until you reveal it to us
We tremble at your roar
We cannot refuse your scroll opened to us, O Lord[5]

Hear the seven thunders answer the shout.
We pray for St. John of Patmos, the Theologian
Who trembling as the seven thunders spoke could not write
"Keep secret, and do not write it down."

The earth trembles and shakes.
You lead your people safely along.[6]
Give to the Lord, O child of the Almighty
Give to the Lord glory and power
Glory is due his name
The voice of the Lord hovers over the waters
The thunder is God's glory,
We hear his voice
It is powerful, majestic, and levels the towers of our mind
Like the Pentecost, the voice of the Lord is a flame of fire
His voice is a refiner's fire
It shakes the wasteland of our hearts.
The voice of the Lord strips our souls bare;
We who are his Temple announce his glory
The Lord sits as King forever and gives strength to His people;
The Lord gives us peace.[7]

The angel standing on the circle of the earth reaches to heaven
The time has come
The oath is given
No more delay

---

5. Amos 3:7–8.
6. Psalm 77:18–20.
7. Psalm 29:1–11.

We raise our hands to heaven
No more delay, the Lord will repay
Rejoice with him, O heavens
Let all God's angels worship him.
Rejoice his people, O nations,
He will strengthen the angels.
The battle comes
God will avenge the blood of his servants
Vengeance is his.
The Lord will repay those who despise him
He will cleanse the land for his people[8]

Behold the seventh angel is delayed
God's mystery to be accomplished.
The voice from heaven to us tell
Go and take the scroll opened from the angel standing on earth's circle
We eat the word of God
It is sweet as honey on our lips
But our stomach is bitter

The words of the Lord are true
More precious than gold
Sweeter than honey
Warnings to us, to his servants
Reward is in their obedience[9]

Lax not
We must prophesy again
The nations and kings we must prophesy

Let the words of my mouth, O Lord, find acceptance
O Lord, let the thoughts of my heart before you bow
O Lord, our redeemer
His enemies will one day fall
Destiny shall meet them at their end
The Lord will give justice to his people

8. Deuteronomy 32:40–43.
9. Psalm 19:11–12.

He will free his servants
There will be neither slave nor free[10]

Amen

The Songs of the Sabbath Sacrifice

The ancient liturgist dwelling at Qumran chose one day to record the songs of his people as they gathered in unison on the Sabbath to sing, expecting a mystical experience.[11] Even with history's poor attempt at destroying them, we have managed to find nine of these songs in the Judean desert. These songs (4Q400–7) speak of gods (angels), thrones, heavens, and thunders. Those who dwelled at Qumran, in attempting to reach the mystical sphere, would sing of these angels and their visitations to humans across time. In one, they even sing of seven tongues. "He will sing to the King of Holiness seven times, with se[ven words of wonderful [songs.] Seven psalms of his blessings. Seven ps[alms of magnification of his justice.]."[12] Perhaps John's "seven thunders" (10:4) is an allusion to the angelic tongues heard by God and the Mystic.

Why were the angels so important to the community? The angels are the priests of heaven![13] Because the Qumran community had come to believe the Temple in Jerusalem corrupt, they retreated to the desert. Since Judaism was centered on the Temple, the community began to look elsewhere for their celebrations. They needed priests, a calendar, and a new Temple—the hallmarks of religion. "The calendar of the Community already organized temporality according to the rhythm of the celestial liturgies: community times, sacred and profane, at odds with the Jerusalem calendar, are in unison with the angelic festivities."[14] They looked towards heaven.

10. Deuteronomy 32:1–6.
11. Schiffman, *Reclaiming the Dead Sea Scrolls*, 351–60.
12. Martinez and Tigchelaar, *The Dead Sea Scrolls Study Edition*, 823.
13. Barber, *Coming Soon*, 137.
14. Schmidt, *How the Temple Thinks*, 151.

In the liturgy of St. James, we find a reference to angels as well. "Let all mortal flesh be silent, and stand with fear and trembling, and meditate nothing earthly within itself:—For the King of kings and Lord of lords, Christ our God, comes forward to be sacrificed, and to be given for food to the faithful; and the bands of angels go before Him with every power and dominion, the many-eyed cherubim, and the six-winged seraphim, covering their faces, and crying aloud the hymn, Alleluia, Alleluia, Alleluia."[15] This is preserved in the liturgy of the Orthodox Armenian Church, with a song sung by representatives of the angels right before the Great Entrance. "We who mystically represent the Cherubim, and who sing the thrice holy hymn to the Holy Trinity, let us lay aside all worldly care, that we may welcome the King of Heaven and earth, whom legions of angels escort unseen."[16]

What is this escort? It is union of angels and saints (heaven and earth) to escort the conquering King (1 Thessalonians 4:17) into the chamber. In Divine Liturgy of John Chrysostom this is the Triumphal Hymn, placed after the benediction/invitation and before the work of redemption is recited. In other liturgies, angels are referenced as well.

What do we see here? What are we supposed to feel? John is warning the delay of Christ's coming is at an end. Jesus sends his angel to announce to John the King is ready to enter into the Throne room. We are to feel a moment of excitement, perhaps like Christmas morning, or rather, that moment of anticipation on our wedding day or before that first kiss. We are ready to meet the king, again, for the first time—each and every time.

The moment of anticipation is a time for self-renewal as well. We grow quite weary in our daily prayers and even in taking the

---

15. *The Divine Liturgy of St. James* in *ANF,* 7:540. Traditionally, an early date (60) held for this liturgy, but the best time table is a fourth century dating, allowing for a *creatio ex materia* (i.e., that it developed from an early Tradition to the recognizable form about the fourth century).

16. Hammond, *Liturgies: Eastern and Western*, 149.

The Cherubic Hymn

Eucharist. We become bored with our worship services. This is not uncommon but human. This is our condition and we must learn to accept it. This is why we have these moments of anticipation, to grow that seed of excitement once more. The king is coming! The Trumpets are blaring! Our heart begins to race, our blood pounding. Are we prepared? Have we purified our minds to focus only on Jesus and the Cross? This is the moment to do so, for the delay of Jesus is coming to an end.

A Prayer of Adoration

O God of Heaven, hear our prayer
Send forth your angels
Let heaven and earth join as your royal escort.

Lord, we remember the cloud and the fire of Israel's story.
We remember the rainbow of Noah's flood
We remember the sun you gave as a light to our path
Lord, we yearn for your Scriptures

Stand, O Angel, upon the land and the sea
Stand between heaven and earth and shout!
Let the seven angels shout with you!
Let the mysteries be kept quiet

Swear, O Angel, but the Creator of All Things
Tell us the delay is nearly at the end
Whisper to us of God's soon coming
Show us the appearance of Jesus

It is finished, O My Jesus.
You are nearly here.
Sing to us from your holy writings
We will eat them and be filled
Let us tell of your Gospel to all people

10

The Great Entrance

"For what is that worth which does not beget humility
and charity, mortification, and holy simplicity and silence?"[1]

We see in the first part of this chapter something of a silence. John quietly measures the temple of God while the witnesses of God are proclaiming the message of heaven. The ancient temple was a place for unity with God. Thus, you have those in quiet meditation and those in joyful celebration occupying the same space. So too the forms of prayer taken by mystics.

"Hence it becomes more evident that the fitting disposition for this union is, not that the soul should understand, taste, feel, or imagine anything on the subject of the nature of God, or any other thing whatever, but only that pureness and love which is perfect resignation, and complete detachment from all things for God alone."[2] When John is measuring the Temple, he is not measuring bricks and stones, wood and gold, but that inward temple of the soul. "All this is applicable to those souls who are enlightened by God and in Him transformed. For though it be true that every soul, according to its measure, great or little, may attain to this union, yet all do not in an

1. Saint John of the Cross, *The Ascent of Mount Carmel*, 224.
2. Saint John of the Cross, *The Ascent of Mount Carmel*, 80–1.

equal degree, but only as our Lord shall give unto each; as it is with the blessed in heaven, there some see God more perfectly than others, and yet all see Him and all are satisfied and happy, for each one is filled with the vision according to his merits, greater or less."[3] When John measures his Temple, measure your soul (Philippians 2:12–6).

The First Prayer: Revelation 11:1–14

Do we not trample God's holy city?
For three years Rome marched on Israel
For six years Germany massacred the Jews
For centuries the Church has grieved our brothers and sisters
We trample the holy city, but God has given us a place
In the holy courtyard of the Temple
Where John measures our grace.

Our God, you are not one who delights in evil
The wicked find no peace with you
The arrogant are made humble in your eyes
You, O Lord, hate all evil and destroy the liars
Loathe, Our God, the men of war and death[4]
God will destroy those who destroy his Temple.
Our God's temple is holy
We are his temple.[5]

The Two Witnesses cry out to us
These are two prophets and two olive trees
These two lampstands bow before the Lord
They cannot be harmed
Their enemies are consumed by the fire of their mouths

O Prophet of the Lord speak to us
The Lord says,

---

3. Saint John of the Cross, *The Ascent of Mount Carmel*, 81.
4. Psalm 5:5–7.
5. 1 Corinthians 3:17.

Praying in God's Theater

"My words will flame out of your mouth
They burn the people like kindling wood."[6]

Because we try to harm them
There is a draught upon the land
The rivers and the oceans are turned to blood
The earth is filled with plagues
They have a testimony to us
The beast from the endless abyss will kill
The Two Witnesses will lie like an open book
From Rome and Jerusalem we will laugh at them and their failure

There is no sincerity in our mouth
Our hearts are corrupt
Our throats are an open grave
We lie with every move of our tongue
Declare us guilty, O God
Let us fall by our own devices
Drive us away for our many sins
We have rebelled against you[7]

God's words have become a relic to us
The whole earth marvels at their death
We will not bury them, only laugh
We celebrate the death of the Two Witnesses
How long have they tormented us?
In God's time, he will breathe life into them

Bring to us the rod of iron
Destroy our godlessness with your word
Rebuke us and let us flee
Reprove us and our hearts
Gather together a holy people and in righteousness lead
Judge the tribes of the earth
Sanctify us by the Lord God
Remove injustice from us

---

6. Jeremiah 5:14.
7. Psalm 5:10–11.

The Great Entrance

We desire to know no wickedness
Let us be the children of God[8]

From heaven God calls the Two Witnesses
Their enemies watch their exaltation
An earthquake strikes
Are we destroyed?

There rock is not our Rock
Their grapes are poison, their clusters bitter
Their wine the venom of snakes
The Lord seals up the blessings until that day
His enemies will one day fall
Destiny shall meet them at their end
The Lord will give justice to his people
He will free his servants
There will be neither slave nor free[9]

Will people ever give glory to God?
The earthquake brings death
The earthquake brings life
We will give glory to the God of heaven

Let everyone glorify the Lord
Let us sing his praise.
The Lord marches forth like a mighty conqueror;
He is dressed in his fury
He crushes his enemies with the shout of victory
He is no longer silent
He no longer restrains himself
Like a woman in labor, the time has come[10]

The second terror is past
See the third terror coming quickly.

---

8. Psalm of Solomon 17:24–27.
9. Deuteronomy 32:31–36.
10. Isaiah 42:12–14.

> We your creation eagerly waits to see God
> His children are revealed.
> Creation was once cursed
> With hope, we look to the day of freedom from the curse
> Creation groans like in pains of childbirth
> Has the time not come?[11]
>
> Amen

The Ministers Prepare

Before the service begins, a priest will clothe himself in the proper garments. In the liturgy of the Orthodox Armenian Church this is a part of the liturgical service, accompanied by singing Psalm 132. It begins,

> Lord, remember David
> and all the adversity he endured,
> how he swore an oath to the Lord
> and made this vow to the Mighty One of Jacob:
> "I will not live in my house
> nor will I go to my bed,
> I will give myself no rest,
> nor allow myself sleep,
> until I find a sanctuary for the Lord,
> a dwelling for the Mighty One of Jacob."

It is fitting that this Psalm, one speaking to a plight of a minister serving in the Temple, is the one performed while preparing for the work of the Lord.

It has become somewhat fashionable of late to discard Tradition, the early Church witnesses, and historical Christian doctrinal stances. Yet we know Christ by the preaching (Tradition) of the Apostles and the Church by the creeds and other canonical elements. To discard them is to remove our anchor to the past and chart our future course only into chaos. Protestants often see the Reformation

---

11. Romans 8:19–22.

The Great Entrance

as a return to a pure view of the Scriptures sans Church Fathers (and thus the Great Tradition). However, if we read these great writers and thinkers—Zwingli, Luther, Calvin and Wesley—we find that they would not desire a complete separation from Church Tradition.

St. Victorinus of Petovium calls the rod of measurement the creed.[12] Others see this as a prophetic revealing regarding the wheat and the tares.[13] Along the same lines, Primasius calls out the "false faith and the contagion of a sinful way of life" emitted by heretics and infecting proper faith.[14] Others such as Andrew of Caesarea and Bede lend their voices not to some dispensationalist (or sensationalist) belief that this is supposedly the Third Temple yet to be built in some far off time, but that this represents the Church of God, the new Temple, and the sin sometimes infecting it. If we are careful to examine our own lives, are we willing to say we are sinless and thus above measurement?

Returning to those who would cast out every sense of Christian doctrine, humility, and morality we must remember John's measuring rod. It is a symbol of authority (Psalm 2; throughout Revelation). In his role as prophet and priest, John has the authority to measure out our sin, with the stress here on out. Are we so vain and arrogant we cannot allow others to tell us of our sins?

There is always a controversy when the Vatican issues statements against giving the Eucharist to those in opposition to canon law. In the United Methodist Church, communion is offered through an open table but with the insistence one has examined his or her own heart before receiving the bread and the wine. What are we to say about these significant differences? Both require us to measure or be measured (Daniel 5:27). Both require us to submit to those invested with spiritual authority, although one forces us to be the impetus of that measurement. Regardless, John's measuring rod is present. Once we have measured or have been measured, we may proceed.

12. St. Victorinus of Petovium, *Commentary on the Apocalypse*, 11.1–2.
13. Matthew 13:24–30; cf., Tyconius, *Commentary on the Apocalypse* 11.1–2.
14. St. Primasius, *Commentary on the Apocalypse*, 11.2.

The Second Prayer: Revelation 11:15–19

Hear the seventh trumpet
The voices of heaven shout
We tremble
We pray
The world is not the Kingdom of our Lord and his Christ
Our Lord and His Christ will reign forever and ever

God will bless those who fear him
The great and the humble
The poor and the wealthy
He will bless all

The elders bow before God and worship him
Let us give thanks to God, the Father, the Almighty
Let us give thanks to the one who is
To the one who always was we give thanks
This one has begun to reign

Bless us, O Lord, us and our children
Bless us, O Lord, you who made the heaven and the earth

Let the nations be filled with wrath for the time has come
Judge, O Lord, the dead and reward the prophets
Reward your holy people
Reward those who fear your name
Destroy those who destroy with injustice

The Heavens belong to you, O Lord
But you have given the earth to us
Let us live evermore
The dead cannot praise the Lord
But the living can
Let us live evermore

Behold the Temple of God stands open in heaven
The Ark of God's People is seen

Praise the Lord both now and forever!

Praise the Lord always![15]

Amen

The Subversive Meal[16]

In the Byzantine Liturgy of the seventh century the Great Entrance is the moment the priest brings in the bread and the wine.[17] We have built to this during the preceding chapters. This is the moment wherein the priest carries in the memorial to our Lord, announced by a trumpet. This may be an invention of later times, from the closing of the Divine Liturgy of Saint James (fourth century) until sometime before the seventh; however, what we can allow is the crescendo of the Eucharist is recognized, whether the elements are present or are brought in by the priest.

Notice the angelic hymn in 11:15: "Sovereignty over the world has passed to our Lord and his Christ, and he shall reign forever." We must not read this divorced of Psalm 2. This is the moment in the liturgical celebration Christ is anointed King! The Son assumes the Throne and is given the rod of iron. This is why the song is now directed to include Jesus! In this moment of our Eucharistic celebrations we proclaim Jesus victorious over the princes of the air (Ephesians 6:12). He has won us our freedom from sin!

We return again to Boxall's "theatre of reception." His point is made dramatically clear in 11:16–18 when the Thanksgiving Hymn is sung. "It is precisely in the Eucharist that the End breaks into the present, as the Lamb's marriage feast is anticipated. So too in this eucharistic prayer of the heavenly elders . . . the Lord's coming

---

15. Psalm 115:13–18.

16. The title for this subsection comes from Streett's *Subversive Meals*. His work has influenced some of this section. See also Koenig, *The Feast of the World's Redemption*.

17. Brightman, *Liturgies: Eastern and Western*, 535.

Praying in God's Theater

judgement is made present."[18] Why? Why should you consider this hymn, at time moment, related to the Eucharist?

R. Alan Streett calls the Eucharist a subversive meal because it refused to honor Caesar; instead, it honors Jesus as the head of the world. When the early Christians acted out the divine drama, it was not to Caesar they rendered an oblation, but to Jesus as Lord. The very act of the Eucharist becomes a hidden transcript whereby the ancient community could communicate the mysteries of the faith—Jesus is Lord; Caesar is not! Possibly, this is a reason why we read in the ancient liturgies the catechumens were dismissed before the Eucharist. The meal, an essential element in early Christianity, was their emblem of resentence to Rome. "The Last Supper is a literary Janus culminating the sequence of Jesus' earthly meals but already strongly anticipating the table fellowship in his resurrected state (Luke 24:30, 43)."[19]

The last few verses help in understanding this as the Eucharistic entrance. How is this possible? Our theology is not *ex nihilo*, but *ex materia*. We understand the meaning of this passage because we have seen it before in the story of Jacob's ladder (Genesis 28:10–19), in the Gospels, and now in John's work. The ladder is Jesus in his role as mediator between God and his Creation (1st Timothy 2:5). Because of his, during our Eucharistic celebrations we through Christ are gathered to heaven. "The community in the church on earth is mystically gathered at God's altar on high."[20] Thus, as the body and the bloody make their way to the altar, we are shown a glimpse of heaven's inner sanctum wherein lies the fabled Ark of the Covenant.

It is not surprising to see the earliest Christian worship manual, the Didache, has a prayer connecting the Eucharist with the Ark. Nicholas Perrin translates Didache 10.2 as, "We give you thanks, Holy Father, on account of your holy name which you have caused to pitch a tent in our hearts." Perrin writes, "As a eucharistic prayer,

---

18. Boxall, *The Revelation of Saint John*, 170.
19. Hahn, *Kinship by Covenant*, 222.
20. Turner, *At the Supper of the Lamb*, 89.

The Great Entrance

this can only be drawing an implicit analogy between the believers' partaking of the Eucharist and the tabernacle high priests' ingesting the Bread of the Presence."[21] Again, we see an early Christian theological belief of the thin place united by prayer and the Eucharist.[22]

In an older version of the oldest Eucharist prayer in Rome, we see this belief encapsulated rather neatly:

> In humble prayer we ask you, almighty God:
> command that these gifts be borne
> by the hands of your holy Angel
> to your altar on high in the sight of your divine majesty,
> so that all of us, who though this participation
> at the altar receive the most holy Body and Blood of your Son,
> may be filled with every grace and heavenly blessing.[23]

We are not yet ready to partake of the Eucharist, but the anticipation grows. This is a goal of contemplative unity, to draw us closer to God in anticipation of the certain unity.

What do we make of this for our individual prayers? What is given for us is the notion first of measuring out our souls, to see if they are acceptable to God. Second, we know the altar is laid down before us. With the altar in view, we know as well the coming reign of Jesus as expressed through the Eucharist is near. In chapter 10, we were promised no more delay; in chapter 11, we are singing about the immediate reign of Jesus. Yet, the Eucharist is not yet laid out. Are we too wretched to partake? Hardly. Rather, let us consider the thin places and how time works here.

We are united to God through our prayer and the Eucharist. We are given a special vantage point to watch as the world goes by. We should not forget, however, we are near Eternity. While we are still time bound, God is not. Further, what we must draw from this is God does not just inhabit the bread and the wine, but requires our

---

21. Perrin, *Jesus the Temple*, 50.

22. Prayer is likewise a symbol of resistance. When we seek petitions of God we are showing allegiance to someone other than the Emperor.

23. We should not so easily forget the entirety of the Epistle to the Hebrews as well.

continual praise. Why is this? Psalm 22:3 reads, "You, the Praise of Israel, are enthroned in the sanctuary." We enthrone (again, call to mind Psalm 2) God by our praise. The Eucharist is the living symbol of the victory of God, but it is by our praise (and our praises through our prayers) God is enthroned.

This is not a sign God is dependent upon us, as God will always have someone to praise him. Rather yet, think of it this way. We acknowledge through our prayers he is God alone. We enthrone him no longer in an earthly temple, but as John begins this chapter by noting, in the Temple of flesh and blood. We need not wait for the presence of the body and the blood to praise God, or to know Jesus is Lord, but we acknowledge this when we bend the knee to Heaven.

The Ark of the Covenant is equally important as an image connecting us immediately to the next chapter. Examine for yourself Luke 1 where we read the Holy Spirit overshadows Mary. This language is intentional. "The Greek word for 'overshadow' is the same word used to describe God's presence 'overshadowing' the ark in the tabernacle in the Old Testament."[24] Consider this as we move one.

A Prayer of Adoration

> O God, your Church is the Temple
> We are your Temple
> Measure out our souls
> Find them worthy,
> Make them worthy, O God
>
> Teach us through your Scriptures
> Bring together the Old and the New
> Give us our daily bread
> Let us place ourselves on the altar of your word

---

24. Barber, *Coming Soon*, 148.

The Great Entrance

Great God, our kingdoms are yours
My mind, heart, and soul are yours
You and your Anointed will reign forever.

We give thanks to you, O God Almighty
Take your power and reign
Let the heathens rage at your wrath
Judge the living and the dead
Reward the righteous; punish the wicked

Show us your Temple, O God
Give sight so that we may see the covenant
Tabernacle in our hearts, Great God.

11

The Presentation of Israel, the Church, and Mary

"Holy Mary, Mother of God, pray for us sinners, now and at the hour of our death."[1]

One of the most difficult issues for modern Protestants to accept is the *right* role of Mary in the Christian story. When we read of the Immaculate Conception, the Perpetual Virginity or the veneration of Mary, we are often aghast at such doctrines, believing them to be the sole domain of either the Roman Catholic Church or the East; yet, many Protestant Reformers—Zwingli, Luther, Calvin and even John Wesley—expressed a belief in some, if not all of the normative Marian doctrines. It is not an eisegetical fallacy to incorporate Mary into the exegetical framework of this chapter. Perhaps it is not given to us today to understand or accept such an exalted view of Mary, but as Zwingli said, "The more the honor and love of Christ increases among men, so much the esteem and honor given to Mary should grow."[2]

Moreover, St. Bonaventure writes,

1. This is the second refrain from the Roman Catholic Rosary.
2. Stakemeier, *De Mariologia et Oecumenismo*, 456.

The Presentation of Israel, the Church, and Mary

If you could perceive the splendor and magnitude of this flame sent down from heaven, the refreshing breeze that came down with it, the consolation it poured forth; if you could understand the loftiness of Mary's elevation, the glorification of humanity, the condescension of divine Majesty; if you could hear the Virgin singing her delight; if you could accompany her into the hill country and witness how the woman who had been barren embraced her and greeted her with words by which the tiny servant recognized his Lord, the herald announced the Judge, the voice proclaimed the Word—oh, surely then, together with the Blessed Virgin, you would most sweetly sing this holy canticle: "*My soul magnifies the Lord . . .* ;" surely, then, together with the infant prophet, you would joyfully and jubilantly adore the marvel of the virgin conception.[3]

The First Prayer: Revelation 12:1–9

Witness the great event in heaven
Behold the woman clothed with the sin
She stands on the moon
She is crowned with twelve stars
She labors with a child
She is ready to give birth

The sun, moon, and eleven stars bow before the chosen son[4]
Praise the wonders of the Lord, O Heavens
Stand with the Lord, You Angels and You Saints
Who in the heavens is equal with God?
Who is like our Lord among the other gods?
The angels and the saints reverence our God
O God of Heaven, who is like you?
O Lord, your promises are sure[5]

---

3. Saint Bonaventure, "Mystical Opuscula," 105–6.
4. Genesis 37:9.
5. Psalm 89:6–9.

Praying in God's Theater

Behold another heavenly event
There is a rebellion in heaven
There is a red dragon, with seven heads crowned and ten horns
By his tail he brings down a third of the angels of God
He stands as midwife, but ready to kill
He seeks to devour and destroy the chosen son.

Jesus is born in Bethlehem
The King pretends peace but readies for war
A star guides, the mother and son abide
We follow this star with joy
The wise are warned against the king
Before the king strikes
Our God sends the Holy Family to Egypt to rest[6]

A son is born who is to rule all nations with an iron rod.
For a time her son is taken by the dragon, dead
But God on his throne rescues him

We hear the Lord who declares
He along places the king chosen on the throne
The king on the holy mountain in Jerusalem
We hear the Lord again
You are my son; today I am your father
Ask O Blessed Son ask for the nations
Seek us as your possession
Break us and smash our bonds like jars of clay[7]

We pray that the woman flees the dragon
We pray for the place God has prepared for her
There is a war in heaven.

Saint Michael the Archangel,
Defend us in battle.
Be our protection against the wickedness and snares of the devil.
May God rebuke him, we humbly pray;
Thou, O Prince of the Heavenly Host -

---

6. Matthew 2.1–13.
7. Psalm 2.6–9.

The Presentation of Israel, the Church, and Mary

By the Divine Power of God -
Cast into hell, Satan and all the evil spirits,
Who roam throughout the world seeking the ruin of souls.[8]

Heaven thunders as Michael fights the dragon
Angels against angels until the dragon is defeated
To the earth the dragon is cast
To the earth is thrown the devil, Satan, our enemy
On the earth he roams to deceive.

From Eden the devil was clothed with the riches of God.
God gave his authority, set his as guard
Daily the devil wandered the holy mountain
Satan was one perfect until he turned to him
With violence the devil sinned
His riches too tempting to satisfy him
His heart was filled with pride, his wisdom destroyed
He was thrown to earth, naked and exposed
The kings of the earth defiled themselves with him
He brought injustice and was consumed by sin
But his fate is assured
He will come to a dreadful finish
He will exist no more[9]

Amen

The Hymn of the Lady

One needs not be completely convinced this passage is about Mary. We can acknowledge the role of a woman in this passage, but allow this woman could be one of the various "good" women in Scripture.[10] We may allow this woman is Israel and equally proclaim this is the

---

8. This is composed from the prayer to St. Michael the Archangel.

9. Ezekiel 28:13–19.

10. Scripture is often condemned as having but one view of women. This is a sadly poor exegetical attempt. Proverbs, for example, gives evidences of both the good woman and the bad woman. Likewise, is treated as an evil woman while Judah is the good woman.

Church, both assigned the feminine gender in Holy Writ. Or, we may combine each of these sentiments and see this as Mary, albeit a theologized Mary, imbued with the holiness of Israel and the nascent Church. As Barber (above) has shown, there is covenantal language in Mary's *Magnificent* where Luke pictures her as enjoining not just the divine and the human in the Incarnation, but so too Israel and now the Gentiles.

Consider as well the story of Jesus in the Gospels who is transformed as the embodiment of Israel. Where they were disobedient, he is obedient. Where they were the faithless children, he is the faithful son. If the story of Jesus is theologized in this way, cannot we say the same for Mary? Indeed, this is the circular development of theology we have experienced thus far. Perhaps Revelation 12 has influenced in some way later Marian theology, just as later Marian theology now influences us in how we see this chapter.

We have an allowance from history to understand how Mary fitted neatly into John's liturgical drama and subsequent ecclesiastical developments. Are we pressed to see Mary here? St. Ignatius of Antioch, among other early Christian writers, mentions Mary in his epistle to the Ephesians. The early Christian writers did not forget her and while we may see something of a growth in Marian theology in the later centuries, it is because (like the Trinity and other developed Christian doctrines) they found seeds in the New Testament. The role of Mary is even enshrined in our baptismal liturgies. "Do you believe in Jesus Christ, the Son of God, who was born of the Virgin Mary by the Holy Spirit," is a question asked in a third century forerunner of the Apostle's Creed.[11]

Mary is present in the earliest liturgies as well. In the Divine Liturgy of St. James, we read "Hail, Mary, highly favoured: the Lord is with Thee; blessed art thou among women, and blessed the fruit of thy womb, for thou didst bear the Saviour of our souls."[12] More

---

11. Evans and Wright, *The Anglican Tradition*, 16.
12. *The Divine Liturgy of James* in *ANF,* 7:546.

conducive to our current prayers, we turn again to the Liturgy of the Armenians and begin were we left off above.

After the preparation for the Great Entrance is given and performed, there is another part of the celebration called the *Prothesis*, the part of the service where the altar is prepared. It is "(t)he office or act of setting forth the oblation, including the arrangement of the bread on the paten, the mixing of the chalice and the veiling."[13] As we have seen this in chapters 10 and 11, we are now ready to see the other part of the *Prothesis*, the hymn to Mary.

> Rejoice greatly, O Zion, daughter of light, holy mother-church with thy children: adorn and embellish thyself, O fair spouse and heavenlike sanctuary, for the anointed God, being of being, is ever sacrificed in thee unconsumed in reconciliation of the Father and distributeth his own body and blood in expiation of us for the fulfilment of his dispensation
>
> May he grant forgiveness to the founder of this temple The holy church confesseth the pure virgin Mary mother of God, from whom hath been given us the bread of immortality and the cup of rejoicing. Give ye him blessings in spiritual songs.[14]

Immediately what we see is the union of interpretations. The Church sings to Israel; the congregation to the Church; and all to Mary as one. Mary has, in the Liturgy, come to represent the union of the "good" feminine trope in Scripture. She is both Israel and the Church, standing as the middle between the two supposedly opposing forces. What Mary does in both Scripture and in ancient liturgies is to give birth to a new reality in the fruit of her womb. While we may seek to temper a high view of Mary, we must remain ever so watchful we do not completely dismiss her role in God's plan of salvation.

---

13. Brightman, *Liturgies: Eastern and Western*, 586.
14. Brightman, *Liturgies: Eastern and Western*, 420–1.

Perhaps John did not mean to write it as such, but through the inspiration of the Spirit, a Marian image may have been placed. Perhaps this is why we find Mary mentioned in the Apostle's Creed, other early baptismal liturgies, the above-mentioned liturgies as well as the liturgies from the Syrian and the Coptic Jacobite Churches and the Orthodox Armenian Church among others. The ancient liturgies are drawing from Revelation; therefore, it is not impossible to allow for a Marian understanding of this chapter, even if we must equally recognize it is heavily theologized.

The Second Prayer: Revelation 12:10–18

Behold the voice from heaven
Salvation at last!
The power of the kingdom of God at last!
The authority of Christ, at last!
There stands no more accuser of the Church!

Behold the ransomed of the Lord!
They return to Jerusalem and Zion
Let us enter singing our everlasting joy
For distress and lament has vanished
Behold Christ has brought us joy and gladness[15]

By the Blood of the Lamb
By our Witness to Jesus,
Satan is defeated
What is our life that is not in Jesus?
Rejoice, O heavens!
Rejoice you citizens of heaven!
Watch carefully, you citizens of the earth
Watch for the devil prowls with great anger and little time

O Precious Blood of Jesus,
Infinite price of creation's redemption,
Both drink and laver of our souls,

15. Isaiah 51:11.

Plead always our cause before the throne of infinite mercy;
From the depths of our heart, we adore you,
Who would not bless this Blood of endless worth?
Who does not feel within themself the fire of Jesus's love?
What is our fate without this blood of redemption?
From the last drop is it is drawn from the veins of our Savior
This is the work of love.
O infinite love, which has given us this saving balm!
O balm beyond all price,
Welling up from the fountain of infinite love,
Grant that every heart and every tongue may be enabled to praise you,
Let every heart magnify you
Let every soul give you thanks both now and for evermore.
Amen.[16]

The dragon does not stop his pursuit
Emboldened by his diseased outcast
He pursues the birth of the only son
Behold the mother who is given wings to fly away
She hides in the wilderness in God's time and care

We remember God found Israel in a wasteland.
He protected them with his arms
He guarded them as his own body
Like an eagle over her chicks he spread his wings, carrying them
The Lord alone protected them[17]

The dragon is not content with God's protection
See the dragon as he tries to drown with red waters Israel
But the earth opens up and swallows the rivers
God protects his people

Awake, arise, O Lord!
Cover yourself with strength!
Flex your mighty right arm!

---

16. This is composed from the prayer known as the *O Precious Blood of Jesus* prayer, instituted by Pope Pius VII in 1815.

17. Deuteronomy 32:10–12.

Praying in God's Theater

> **Awake as in ancient times when you killed Egypt, the Nile's dragon**
> **It was you who dried up the sea**
> **It was you who made the path of escape on the bottom of the sea**[18]

> But the dragon does not repent but declares war on the woman and her son
> First against Israel and then the Church
> Against all the prophets and the apostles
> Against those who keep God's commandments and the witness of Jesus
> Behold the dragon as he takes his stand on the sea's shore

> O Dragon, have you forgotten the Lord?
> Your Creator is the one who has stretched out the sky
> He has laid the foundations of the earth
> We will not remain in fear of our oppressors
> The anger of our enemies does not frighten us
> Their terror and wrath have disappeared
> The captives will be released
> We will not suffer; we will not die!
> We do remember our Lord![19]

> Amen

The Birth Was Not Enough

A Jewish hymn song near Passover, the *Dayeinu*, recounts the story of Israel. At the ending of each event–verse, the singer shouts *dayeinu*! It suffices! It is a rhetorical poem, recounting one act of God's grace, followed by a proposal that had the second act not happened, it would still suffice. For example, if God had only brought Israel out of Egypt, but not brought justice upon the Egyptians, *dayeinu*! It is doubtful the song's intent is what the surface level portrays; instead, the song is meant to recount God's blessings while praising God for each one in particular.

---

18. Isaiah 51:9–10.
19. Isaiah 51:13–14.

The Presentation of Israel, the Church, and Mary

Sadly, our Western Christian traditions now seem to revolve around the birth of Christ, celebrated joyfully and perhaps a bit sacrilegiously in December. When Easter appears, there is something of a small remembrance, but it does not contain the level of frivolity of the previous holiday. Many would think these are the only days in the Christian calendar, with the preference given to the image of the Baby Jesus. This is the human Jesus, the one we can relate to, the one we can use as an excuse to receive gifts from our loved ones. Indeed, many see the birth as simply *dayeinu*!

Scripture tells us otherwise. The Apostle Paul, writing his letters feverishly to churches in Asia, focused on the death, burial, and resurrection of Jesus Christ. Mark (the earliest Gospel) and the John (the final canonical Gospel) both skip the birth of Jesus and instead focus on his death and resurrection. The birth matters, but a birth of a Jewish prophet was rather commonplace. However, it is the resurrection that sets Jesus a part. It is his death and resurrection, not his birth, that secures for us our Christian liberty. If the Gospel is simply the birth of a good man, we should read the Gospels as a tragic story of child abuse by a wrathful God-father, who simply wished his son to die. But, the focus of the Gospel story is on the final few hours of Jesus. It was not enough for Jesus to be born and thus be the moral example for us, but he had to die and then be resurrected.

A Prayer of Adoration

> O Lord, let us not deceive ourselves
> You have given us signs in heaven
> We see the good woman in the clouds
> The sun clothes us and the moon gives her comfort
> She is crowned with twelve stars
> And she gives birth
>
> O God, in your great drama, you have given us another sign
> We see the great red dragon
> We'll see this dragon again

Here, he attacks the woman
O Great God, reveal to us these signs

O Great God, because of the war in heaven
Satan was cast down. Here he wages war against you
But you sent us Israel
Through Israel you sent us the Virgin
Through the Virgin and the Holy Spirit you sent us your Son

Let us praise the salvation that has come
Praise to the power and to the kingdom of our God
Praise to the authority of Christ who vanquishes the devil
Praise to the saints who cover the great dragon

Rejoice you heavenly host, for our God reigns
Rejoice you saints, for our God reigns
Keep well this testimony of Jesus.

12

The Presentation of the Church Triumphant

"Christianity is at its greatest when it is hated by the World."[1]

Who would fear a small group following a crucified criminal? What exactly causes the Beast to wage war against them? The earliest Christians were known as those who appealed to the poor and oppressed, often times taking in abandoned children, caring for the widows, and showcasing the love of Christ.

Is this really politically dangerous? Maybe, but more than likely the cause of war here is to deny Caesar his status as god and lord. If we say Jesus is Lord, we are saying (even if it is only by silence) Caesar is not. In the lead-up to the Jewish Revolt against Rome (66–73), the treasonous act causing Rome to invade was not attacks on citizens, but the refusal to allow for prayers in the Temple for Caesar. The World System, i.e., Rome, was directly challenged. When we say Jesus is our Lord and God (John 20:28), we are ending our allegiance to Rome, replacing temporal authorities with the heavenly one, and surrendering ourselves only to God.[2]

1. St. Ignatius, Bishop of Antioch in his letter to the Roman church
2. See the discussion above on how the Eucharist as well accomplishes this.

Praying in God's Theater

While we may yet remain mortal, we are reminded our ultimate concern is not election cycles or government participation, but the immortal. Once we visibly make this break, we will attract the notice of the earthly authorities. How dare we give allegiance to God first and they only second? We celebrate this allegiance in our prayers and our liturgical celebrations when we mark ourselves out as one who is loyal to a higher authority.

The direction of our worship marks us for our allegiance. If we step back and examine this passage from a good distance, we do not see a diagram of a war machine, but that of the war of words.

Worshiping words.

Liturgies.

The worshipers of God are compared to the worshipers of the Dragon, but the battle is not physical. Rather, the battle is very much a war of words springing from the heart. If our lips give only a shape to the words, then it is fruitless. Yet, if the liturgies and our words in prayer spring up from our innermost parts, our victory is assured.

The First Prayer: Revelation 13:1–10

We see a beast rising out of the sea
Seven heads and ten horns, crowned all
We hear the blasphemies against God from each head
The beast looks like a leopard with feet from a bear and the roar of a lion
It does not have power by itself, but from the dragon

Let the people of God behold Behemoth, made of God.
It is the example of all of God's creation
Only God can tame him
The mountains feed him, the plants shade him
Behemoth is not disturbed by anything
Only God can pacify him.[3]

---

3. Job 40.15–24.

Cheer as one of the heads is wounded
Mourn as the fatal wound is healed!
The world will marvel at its own power
It will be loyal to the beast!
They see no one greater
Behold the beast as it blasphemes God!

Let the People of God give thanks
God is always e near.
Let the people tell of the Lord's works.
In God's time, he has planned
In God's time, he will bring justice against the wicked

Behemoth blasphemes God
In the Temple he slanders God and the Saints

When the earth is moved
When the people live in terror
It is God who keeps the foundations fixed
He warns the proud of boasting
He warns the wicked of defiance

But the beast conquers us, O Lord
He rules over us, Babel's descendants
The people around us worship the Beast
Their names are not written in the Book of Life
This book belongs to the Lamb slain
Before the world began this book was written

Let no one—from the east to the west
Let no one here or there
Let no one in the city or the wilderness
Raise a fist to defy God
God alone judges
God alone decides our course
The Lord's hand holds our cup
For the righteous, it is blessings
For the wicked, it is judgment[4]

---

4. Psalm 75.

> Let those with a heart for God understand
> Anyone whose course it is to suffer will suffer
> If the course is to die, they will die
> Let the people of God endure all patiently
> Let the people of God remain faithful
>
> **We pray for the strength to obey the words of Jesus**
> **We will stand before governors and rulers**
> **To proclaim the Gospel we take every moment**
> **Arrests are not persecution, but chances**
> **We will respond not with fear but with the Gospel**
> **God will give us the words**
> **The Father will speak through us**
> **We will remain faithful**[5]
>
> Amen

War of Words

As in the unnatural break between chapters 11 and 12, there is a continuous move of thought from 12 to 13. Examine different bible translations and you will see 13.1 playing different roles. For some, this is John standing on the seashore and thus rightly a part of chapter 12. Others imply it is the dragon on the shore. I believe the former is preferable and will be assumed for this chapter. The original author, free of the modern imposition of chapters and verses, wrote a long and winding passage, traipsing through the thin places of heaven and earth, past and present (much of the language here is in the present tense). We too move from Heaven to Earth, from the past (the Gospel) to the present (the witness of the Saints).

During the Liturgy of the Blessed Apostles, we find a moment when the priest or minister says a prayer for those who are oppressed,

> O Lord God Almighty, accept this oblation for the whole Holy Catholic Church, and for all the pious and righteous fathers who have been pleasing to Thee, and for all the

---

5. Matthew 10:18–20.

The Presentation of the Church Triumphant

prophets and apostles, and for all the martyrs and confessors, and for all that mourn, that are in straits, and are sick, and for all that are under difficulties and trials, and for all the weak and the oppressed, and for all the dead that have gone from amongst us; then for all that ask a prayer from our weakness, and for me, a degraded and feeble sinner. O Lord our God, according to Thy mercies and the multitude of Thy favours, look upon Thy people, and on me, a feeble man, not according to my sins and my follies, but that they may become worthy of the forgiveness of their sins through this holy body, which they receive with faith, through the grace of Thy mercy for ever and ever. Amen.[6]

This liturgical détente between the child from Revelation 12 and the dragon following him and us throughout this book is coming to a close. Here, we celebrate the Son while "all the inhabitants of the earth" worship the dragon. Perhaps this is hyperbolic, with too many "alls" thrown around; however, from the earliest Christian history we see the use of the a dualistic symbolism. While we have a positive dualism such as the two powers in heaven (early Christology), two hands of God (Irenaeus and Theophilius of Antioch), and the two Testaments of the Canon (Tertullian) there are negative dualisms as well. Not only did Gnosticism present a false dichotomy between flesh and spirit but early Christians envisioned two ways, one evil and one good (the *Didache* and *Epistle of Barnabas*). What John sees here is two forms of worship, the good and the wrong.

In Revelation 13 there are several possible references to the passion of Jesus Christ. First, we see the Roman Emperor (the dragon), Pilate (the beast), as well as a reference to the garden scene in Matthew 26:52 (compare Revelation 13:10). Might we identify with Jesus as martyrs? Ignatius, the third bishop of Antioch did. In his Epistles he writes of his desire to be proved a Christian by martyrdom. Some may see this as a death wish, but Ignatius is simply acting out the Baptismal Union. In Romans 6, Paul compares baptism to dying

---

6. *The Liturgy of the Blessed Apostles* in *ANF,* 7:564–65.

with Christ. How, then, can we not see the life of a Christian as one called to such a course?

St. John of the Cross writes,

> Again: let us suppose a man longing for martyrdom, to whom God shall say, 'Thou shalt be a martyr.' Upon this such an one feels great interior consolation, and hopes of being a martyr. Still he does not die a martyr's death, and yet the promise is fulfilled. But why is the promise not literally performed? Because God keeps it in the highest and substantial sense, bestowing on that soul the essential love and reward of a martyr, making it a martyr of love, granting to it a prolonged martyrdom of suffering, the continuance of which is more painful than death. Thus He bestows really on that soul what that soul desired, and He had promised. For the substance of that desire was, not any particular kind of death, but rather the oblation to God of the obedience of a martyr, and a martyr's act of love. Martyrdom itself is nothing worth without the friendship of God, Who by other means gives the love, obedience, and reward of a martyr perfectly; and the soul is satisfied as to its desires, though the death of a martyr is withheld from it.[7]

We must take the time to remember all of those who have died in the name of Christ, either figuratively or in reality. From this desire to keep in remembrance the saints who have died come the traditions of the martyrs. It is enshrined in prayers, theology and in, as we have seen, liturgies. Are we that devoid of a connection to ancient Christianity we would forget the Church Triumphant? In Hebrews 11 and 12, these Saints of old are held up as the "great cloud of witnesses" surrounding us as we progress our own journey of faith. Perhaps we should not shirk them in our daily prayers and liturgical celebrations.[8]

7. Saint John of the Cross, *The Ascent of Mount Carmel*, 165.

8. "The Marian dimension of the christological feasts was made visible. Then, in addition, come the commemorations of the apostles and martyrs and,

The Presentation of the Church Triumphant

The Second Prayer: Revelation 13:11–19

O Lord is the first beast not enough?
Will we die with this second beast?
This beast comes from the earth
He has horns like a lamb but the voice of the dragon
He rules like the first beast
But he has power and miracles
From heaven, fire reigns down
The people of this world worship him

Let the people of God remember Leviathan
No hunter can capture it; no one disturbs it
But all under heaven belongs to God
Behold the Leviathan, with armor impenetrable
From its mouth, it flashes lightning and fire
From its nose, smoke drifts
Leviathan brings terror wherever it goes
The might are afraid of it
It cannot be stopped by sword or weapon known or unknown
The Leviathan has no equal, no creature as fearful
It is the king of all beasts[9]

Be not deceived by the Leviathan
Only the people of this world worship him
They fall down at the trumpet of the stature to worship
The people of this world worship the created more than the Creator
Leviathan feeds those who are marked as his
Behemoth and Leviathan would starve the people of God
But God numbers them
Known to us, this mystery
Because our heart is towards God

---

finally, the memorials of the saints of every century." (Ratzinger, *The Spirit of the Liturgy*, 111.) It is no accident Ratzinger connected the "Marian dimension" to the commemoration of the martyrs. He notes in the chapter cited herein that the evolution of the direction of worship began with the Eucharistic Altar and the tomb of the martyr, writing that martyrdom is the same "self-oblation" as Christ (75–77).

9. Job 41:1.

> Let the people of God proclaim God's works
> Let us since the praises of Israel's God
> God will break the Behemoth
> God will tame the Leviathan
> He will give us strength to over come[10]

> Amen

The End of Agony

St. Bonaventure writes, "Now that the agony of the passion was over, and the bloody dragon and the savage lion thought they had obtained victory by murdering the Lamb, the power of divinity began to shine forth in His soul descending into hell. Through this power, our strong *Lion of the tribe of Juda*, rising against His fully armed foe, tore away its prey, broke down the gates of hell, and shackled the serpent. *Disarming the Principalities and Powers, He displayed them openly, leading them away in triumph.* Now Leviathan has been led about with a hook, his jaw pierced by Christ Himself."[11]

We are not yet at the end of our agony. The final portion of this chapter moves towards the extreme fear Christians have had since it was written, that somehow we would be marked by the beast or perhaps left in the lurch when all others are marked in such a way and unable to defend ourselves. Our anxiety in this regard has left many of us looking quite foolish over the past two millennia.

This is the wrong reading of Revelation, but it is a reading fueling the fires of our imagination. Instead, we must carefully read to understand John is not promising us abandonment, but moving us slowly forward through the plight of his day. War and devastation had enveloped his land. It was not just the Jewish Revolt, but so too the Roman Civil War leaving a trail of death, carnage, and the sting of hopelessness in its wake. How else could he feel, but abandoned? Even Christ, as St. Bonaventure points out, felt this way. "Hence, the

10. Psalm 75:1–13.
11. Saint Bonaventure, "Mystical Opuscula," 132.

One who cannot possibly be derelict cries out that He is forsaken, because many of His members are to suffer distress to the point of appearing almost abandoned by God."[12]

Let us close this chapter with that same sense of abandonment. God has left us alone, to be the object of war, to be defeated, and to rest under the authority of the dragon. We are called to service as martyrs, but told this needs to be only through love. How can we love when we feel unloved? We are in prison, alone and starved. We can only better ourselves by surrendering to the liturgy of the world system where the Eucharistic Altar is the store clerk's counter; the censers filled with prayers of the saints discarded and replaced with loud, blaring ads driving us to consumerism; and where God is replaced with our own selfish appetites. This is the liturgy of the world system, where we buy gold that rusts, water that causes thirst, and clothes devoured by moths.

A Prayer of Supplication

Stand, John, on the shore and watch
See the great dragon and beast
Watch them devour the people of God
They wreck us with war
We consume their pride

We rot, from the inside
We have purchased that marked by evil
The world has conquered us and we welcomed it
We have sold God's authority to the Dragon

Saints above, the great cloud of witnesses
See us in our plight and stand beside us
Guide us by your lives
Let us attain to that better perfection

Behold the Dragon wages war against us
He speaks evil against God

12. Saint Bonaventure, "Mystical Opuscula," 177–78.

Praying in God's Theater

>He destroys the Church and the Saints
>He labors against Heaven
>He has overcome the Saints
>
>Those who are fated for prison go
>Those who are fated to die, die
>But we will persevere
>Strengthen our Faith, Oh Great God

13

The Presentation of Jesus

"Behold the Lamb of God! He takes away the sins of the world!"[1]

The first advent of Christ was two-fold. In the first part, celebrated in the festive seasons of Advent and Christmastide, we encounter the earthly Jesus who will die. The second part is celebrated Easter morning when the Christ of life and faith appears. The ancient liturgy recorded by St. Hippolytus theologizes this moment in writing, "who, when he was given over to his voluntary suffering, that he might destroy death and break the bonds of the devil, and tread hell under foot, and enlighten the righteous, and establish the limit of hell, and manifest the resurrection."[2] When we encounter Jesus in chapter 14, he is no less than the one who defeated death in the tomb and is seen in the Resurrection.

The First Prayer: Revelation 14:1–5

Behold the Lamb on Mount Zion!
He stands there with an army marked by the Father's name!

---

1. John 1:29.
2. Evans and Wright, *The Anglican Tradition*, 15.

Behold, the Army of our God!
How great is the Lord!
Behold the holy mountain of our God
In the city of our God!
O Jerusalem; O Zion!
How great is our God, greatly to be praised
Let the whole earth rejoice to see our God
This is the city of the great King! [3]

We hear heaven sounding like oceans roar!
Hear heaven's thunder!
It is the great angel band

It is God himself walking Jerusalem's towers
Behold it is our God who defends the great city
Let the kings of the earth join together and besiege us
For it is God himself who protects us

Hear now the angel band the heavenly choir
They sing before the throne of God
Before the four creatures and the elders they sing praises to God
Let only God's army now learn the song
Let only the redeemed of the earth now learn the song

The kings of the earth flew in terror and pain
Our God has destroyed them with his thunder
We in darkness heard of the city's glory
But now we see it for ourselves
This is the city of the Great King
It is the city of our God and he protects it
Our God, let us think always upon your endless love
O God, our God, let us always worship in your Temple

Behold how holy is God's army
They are blameless and true
Like sheep, they follow him wherever he may go
He has redeemed them from among all people
They are the offering to God and his Lamb

3. Psalm 48.1–2.

O God, we praise your name
All people will praise you
Your right hand has brought you victory
Let Mount Zion rejoice, let Jerusalem sing
We will be glad in your justice.
Let us walk about Jerusalem
We believe God protects the city and Mount Zion
This is our God—this is who our God is
He is our God forever and he will guide us beyond the grave.[4]

Amen

Christ Our Captain

Before the entrance of the elements, the priest in the Syrian Jacobite tradition prays, "With the operation of good works and noble and holy thoughts and the pleasant savour of the true faith and the firstfruits of the gifts of glorious immortal lives be we accounted worthy to offer to the high priest of our confession, even Jesus Christ, a holy and righteous sacrifice for that he of himself hath made purification of our sins and redeemed the world by his sacrifice: whom befitteth glory and honour and worship at this time of the celebration of the divine Eucharist and at all times."[5] We find such prayers directly to Jesus in the Coptic liturgies as well.

However, it is on the Armenian liturgy I wish to focus. With a cry of "draw near!" to the Eucharist, the choir begins to sing, "Mother of faith . . . A marvellous second heaven art thou from glory to glory exalted . . . you who does distribute this spotless bread and gives us to drink this pure blood . . . Come then, O children of the new Zion, meet our Lord in holiness. O Taste and see how gracious our Lord is and mighty! The ancient tabernacle was a type of you, but you are a higher pattern . . . Its leader was Joshua the captain; yours is Jesus the only Son of the Father!"

---

4. Psalm 48:3–14.
5. Brightman, *Liturgies: Eastern and Western*, 80.

And in a loud crescendo, the song ends, "This bread is the body of Christ; this cup is the blood of the new covenant. The greatest of mysteries is revealed to us; God himself is manifested to us herein! This is the same Christ the divine Word who sits at the right hand of the Father and who sacrificed here among us, taking away the sin of the world . . . Now and ever for the time to come and world without end."[6]

Note the connection in the Armenian liturgy between Mary and Jesus. Might the Church in Armenia have received a liturgical design from John's Apocalypse? We may never truly discover how the theological tenants of liturgy were developed in the earliest Church; however, we do have an allowance to see the connection between Mary and Jesus in liturgical prayers. Mary is acknowledged not as a first component, but as the source from which the flesh and blood of Jesus emerged. As before, Mary also takes the place of the Church and Israel in this liturgy.

The scene is one of triumph. Jesus stands on heavenly Mount Zion (Hebrews 12:22) surrounded by the redeemed. Do not stress about the exact number, as numbers do not play a real role in Revelation except to point to the unknown. Suddenly thunders peal, harps play and the choir of the redeemed begin to sing a new song to their king like David would in Psalm 96. Israel's King has won the victory over the great dragon, redeeming by ransom the saved of the earth. Your posture should be one of triumph, realizing it is Christ who has already won our victory, who has already overcome the world. There he stands on Mount Zion, King.

The Second Prayer: Revelation 14:6–13

Behold the Gospel!
Babel's Confusion undone!
The angel of the Lord carries to us this Gospel!
The same Gospel as from the Apostles!
Behold the Gospel!

6. Brightman, *Liturgies: Eastern and Western*, 452–53.

The Presentation of Jesus

Let us hear the beginning of the gospel of Jesus Christ[7]

Let our angels shout, "Fear God!" he shouted.
Give glory to him all people
The Lord sits as judge
Worship the Creator!

Let us sing to the Lord a new song
Let all the earth sing to the Lord
Let us bless his name
He has proclaimed salvation to us!
We will tell of his glory among all![8]

Wake up Babylon!
Another angel swings lo! You have fallen
The great city that wages war against the saints has fallen
All the cities of the world share her guilt
But she alone has fallen

Great is the Lord!
He is feared above all gods
The gods of the nations of naught
It is the Lord who is the Creator
Before him are power and glory[9]
Worship none other

Behold the third angel!
Those who are marked of this world will taste God's wrath
The cup of God's wrath is poured out
Their torment shall be from eternity
They shall stand before the presence of the Lamb slain that they reject

We Gentiles, let us give to the Lord
Give to the Lord all power
Glorify the Lord's name
Let us bring gifts to his Temple

7. Mark 1:1.
8. Psalm 96:1–3.
9. Psalm 96:4–6.

Praying in God's Theater

> We will bow down to the Lord arrayed in holiness
> We tremble before him and declare him as king
> He rules with fairness
> We will not be shaken[10]
>
> God's people must suffer persecution with patience
> Obey his commands, O people of God
> Keep safe your faith in Jesus!
>
> O God have you rejected us?
> Our defenses are broken
> O Lord, are you angry with us?
> The earth is split; the land is ruined
> You have made us suffer persecution
> We have become drunk on the wine of your wrath
> Raise a banner to us
> Give us a wall to face attack
> Rescue your people.
> Save us by your power[11]
>
> Hear a voice from heaven
> Blessed are those who die in the Lord!
> The Spirit calls us blessed who die in the Lord
> For we will rest from our labors
> Our works shall follow us there.
>
> O God, who will bring us to your city?
> Who will lead me from this world?
> No longer reject us, O God!
> Aid us in our battle for only your help is sufficient
> We will win with the help of you, O God
> It is you who destroys our enemies.[12]
>
> Amen

---

10. Psalm 96:7–10.
11. Psalm 60:1–5.
12. Psalm 60:11–14.

The Presentation of Jesus

Three Angels

This passage is filled with angels and anger. God is angry at Babylon, the ancient opponent to God's city. The time for judgment has come. Too often we see God solely as Judge, denying to him his role as Creator and Healer. Judgment is compared to our modern courtroom dramas rather than a Creator judging his Creation good (Genesis 1) or a doctor judging his patient sick and in need of repair. In both Creation (Genesis) and Healing (Revelation) we must see the judgment as connected. God cannot diagnose and heal that which is not his creation. The healing takes place to restore us to the "good" of Creation at the dawn of the Covenant. Judgment has come, but to judge is to repair.

Throughout the Old Testament, God sent his servants to testify to the need for healing. "Thou didst send forth the Prophets; Thou didst perform mighty works by the saints ... who foretold unto us the salvation which was to come."[13] Salvation is not judgmental, but therapeutic.

John Wesley in his sermon, "On the Fall of Man," begins by saying, "Why is there *pain* in the world; seeing God is 'loving to every man, and his mercy is over all his works?' Because there is sin: Had there been no sin, there would have been no pain. But pain (supposing God to be just) is the necessary effect of sin."[14] He continues to explore salvation and healing in this therapeutic sense.[15]

Wesley writes,

> But can the Creator despise the work of his own hands? Surely that is impossible! Hath he not then, seeing he alone is able, provided a remedy for all these evils? Yea, verily he bath! And a sufficient remedy; every way adequate to

---

13. This is part of the silent prayer said by the priest in St. Basil's liturgy. "Basil" in Chrysostom, *The Divine Liturgies of our Fathers*, 357–59.

14. Wesley, *Sermons*, Sermon 57.

15. "For Wesley, the point of Christ's atonement is that human beings, and by extension their societies and cultures, can be healed from the terrible disease of sin, with all its ecological ramifications." (Snyder, *Yes in Christ*, 79).

the disease. He hath fulfilled his word: He bath given "the seed of the woman to bruise the serpent's head."—"God so loved the world, that he gave his only-begotten Son, that whosoever believeth in him might not perish, but have everlasting life." Here is a remedy provided for all our guilt: He "bore all our sins in his body on the tree." And "if any one have sinned, we have an Advocate with the Father, Jesus Christ the righteous." And here is a remedy for all our disease, all the corruption of our nature. For God hath also, through the intercession of his Son, given us his Holy Spirit, to renew us both "in knowledge," in his natural image;—opening the eyes of our understanding, and enlightening us with all such knowledge as is requisite to our pleasing God;—and also in his moral image, namely, "righteousness and true holiness." And supposing this is done, we know that "all things" will "work together for our good." We know by happy experience, that all natural evils change their nature and turn to good; that sorrow, sickness, pain, will all prove medicines, to heal our spiritual sickness. They will all be to our profit; will all tend to our unspeakable advantage; making us more largely "partakers of his holiness," while we remain on earth; adding so many stars to that crown which is reserved in heaven for us.[16]

This therapeutic view is how we may read this chapter. The first angel brings to us the medicine for our disease. These are the everlasting Gospel and the Holy Spirit (springs of water). The second angel tells us of our need for repentance. The third angel brings to us the purging of our sins through our works of grace, separating holy from unholy, clean from unclean, and reminding us our life in Christ includes separation. If we are to be in union with him and thus healed of the separation caused by sin, we must be separated from our sin. When we die in Christ, we are blessed because we are healed.

---

16. Wesley, *Sermons*, Sermon 57.

The Third Prayer: Revelation 14:14–20

O Son of Man, come near on your cloud
O Son of Man, we pray your gold crown is one of victory
We pray your sickle is sharp
We urge you to swing the sickle sharp and remember us
The harvest is here; the earth is ripe

O Son of Man, swing the sickle!
The harvest is ready.
Crush us! Press us! The harvest is ready
The wickedness of the people have filled the earth
In the valley of decision, we wait
The day of the Lord is here.[17]

O my Jesus, swing the sickle sharp
Harvest the whole of the earth.
We behold now your justice
We behold now the other angel with a sickle
This sickle brings justice.
Swing, O Angel, cut the grapes to bring the wine of wrath

Were we but dreaming O God?
Have you restored Zion?
Is Jerusalem filled with joy?
The nations speak of the praises of God
The Lord has done great things
Restore the captives, O God![18]

The justice of God comes with the sickle
The grapes are crushed
Outside the city, the river Jordan is red

O Jesus, my Jesus, we sow in tears
Let us reap in shouts of joy
Let us who carry burdens of sorrow

---

17. Joel 3:13–4.
18. Psalm 126:1–4.

> Return with sheaves of blessings[19]
> The fields of the world are ripe
> O Jesus, send us out, send out your messengers
> Gather your harvest with joy.[20]
>
> Amen

The Harvest Displayed

Once more we have returned to an altar, but now we are gathered to an altar on which lie the essential elements of the Eucharist. There is wheat (v. 15), fire (v. 18), and grapes (v. 19). The Eucharist is continuously presented as the healing salve. Wesley writes, "The grace of God given herein confirms to us the pardon of our sins, by enabling us to leave them. As our bodies are strengthened by bread and wine, so are our souls by these tokens of the body and blood of Christ. This is the food of our souls: This gives strength to perform our duty, and leads us on to perfection."[21]

St. Bonaventure's theology of the Eucharist is intensely breathtaking, and while we should endeavor to explain it fully it is impossible to do so here; however, we may sum up his view of the Eucharist as therapeutic medicine. "Now, because nourishment in the life of grace consists for any one of the faithful in preserving devotion toward God, love for neighbor, and inner delight; and devotion toward God is practiced through the offering of a sacrifice, love for neighbor through union within a single sacrament, and inner delight through partaking of the pilgrim's food: therefore our restoring Principle gave us this sacrament of the Holy Eucharist as a sacrificial offering, as a sacramental union, and as sustainment on the way."[22]

We are limited in our own healing. We may doctor our wounds, but we will find ourselves in need of an amputation rather than a

---

19. Psalm 126:5–6.
20. Matthew 13:38–41.
21. Wesley, *Sermons*, Sermon 101.
22. Saint Bonaventure, "Breviloquium," 253.

return to health. We have seen the outcome of those who worship their own way (Revelation 13, cf. Revelation 16–18). Likewise, we cannot merit enough medicine of our own to heal our souls. "For, after all the efforts of the soul, it cannot by any exertions of its own actively purify itself so as to be in the slightest degree qualified for the Divine union of perfection in the love of God, if God Himself does not take it into His own hands and purify it in the obscure fire."[23]

The fires of the altar represent the love of God. Wesley calls this prevenient grace, or the grace existent in our lives before we feel that draw to Christ. St. John of the Cross writes, "And because occasionally this fire of love grows in the spirit greatly, the longings of the soul for God are so deep that the very bones seem to dry up in that thirst, the bodily health to wither, the natural warmth and energies to perish in the intensity of that thirst of love."[24] Through our prayers we are answering that pull, participating in our heavenly courtship and continuing in the grace drawing us to God. Through our Eucharistic celebrations, we mark that moment when the love of God was manifested for the world.

In the final portion of this chapter, we see the angels commanded by the one who sits on the throne to present the harvest. The wheat, fire, and grapes are thrown to the threshing floor to meet their end. There is no moment in Revelation when the sum of God's people are somehow physically extracted from the earth; however, this is the moment leading to the actual Eucharistic celebration whereby the people of God should find themselves laid upon the altar of God. If we are baptized with Christ, we will suffer with Christ (Romans 6:1–8). If we partake of his body and blood, we will partake of his reward as well (John 6:46–58). We should not fear such a deep examination by God, but stand before the altar with reverence to God while we are judged either ill or healthy. What is the outcome? Regardless, we will be healed.

---

23. Saint John of the Cross, *The Dark Night of the Soul*, 335.
24. Saint John of the Cross, *The Dark Night of the Soul*, 357.

A Prayer of Contrition

Heavenly Father, we behold the Lamb
He is surrounded by the numberless redeemed
They are not marked by sin but are holy

O Great God, heal us of our sins
You have sent your servants to warn us
Our health is in peril
Now send your Son to heal us
Send your Holy Spirit to make us whole

We repent of our immorality
We are drunk on our own power
We have sought to remedy ourselves
We have failed

Yet we rebel against you, O King
We mark ourselves by the Dragon
Purge us of our sins
Give us medicine so that we may be cured

Give us the medicine of our souls, O Son of God
Give us your body and your blood
Let us eat the bread and drink the wine
We will suffer with you and we will live

Amen.

14

The Heavenly Choir

"Here the soul sings of that happy lot, attained by detachment of spirit from all spiritual imperfections, and selfish desires in spiritual things."[1]

There is always a need to sing. "When the unlearned or unbeliever hears us sing triumphant songs to God for our victory over death, when he hears holy Lessons and discourses of the resurrection, when he hears us pray for a happy and joyful resurrection to Glory: by all these he must be convinced, that we do believe the resurrection, which is a principal Article of Christian faith, and the same may be the means to convince him also, and make him believe the same, and so fall down and worship God."[2] While there is the need to sing in accomplishment, there is equally the need to sing in apparent defeat.

I have attempted to thus far cast Revelation as a Eucharistic celebration and as a book from which we may draw connections between ancient liturgies and the stories of our modern lives to build our prayer lives. In this chapter, we see these premises come together and fulfill *lex orandi, lex credenda*. This is John's "new song" he has

1. Saint John of the Cross, *The Ascent of Mount Carmel*, 63.
2. Evans and Wright, *The Anglican Tradition*, 222.

promised us for the last few chapters, a form of worship giving way to theology. It is the mix of voices in harmony with one another and their surroundings singing of God's triumph. There is no defeat here; the opening line cautions us—this is in heaven. Sometimes, the song of freedom cannot be so easily sung on earth, but we must rest assured the liberating choir surrounds us.

Revelation 15:1–8

From heaven's throne see this moment
Seven angels holding tight the seven last plagues
God's wrath is almost complete

We sing to the Lord
It was he who triumphed gloriously;
Both rider and horse is tossed into the sea
The Lord is our defender; he is our song
The Lord has given us the victory
He is our God! Let us praise him! Let us exalt him!
The LORD is my strength and my song; he has given me victory.

O People of God
Stand on the sea of fire
Stand you who are victorious over the world and marked for his name
Hold the harps of the angels
Sing the Song of Moses and the Song of the Lamb
Sing, "Great and wonderful are your works, our God, our Lord, the Almighty."
Sing, "O king of the nations, your ways are true
Your ways are just.
Let all reverence you, O Lord, and praise your name!
Let the nations come and bow before you
Reveal your righteousness to all!

O Lord, your majesty overthrows the rebellious
Consume the wicked with your fury
You have made a way for your people to walk

The waters of our baptism hedge us
Let the enemy chase us with pride
Let the enemy think they can defeat us
O Lord, cover them with water
Let their sins sink deep
Who, O Lord, is like you?
You are glorified in your holiness!

Throw open the doors to the Temple in Heaven!
Let loose the final seven angels!
Let those clothed in spotless linen loose their plagues
They are the wrath of God from eternity
Let the Temple stand empty,
Let there be no more praise, no more repentance
Let the hosts fall silent until the plagues are poured out

Do you hear, O World?
Tremble with anguish
Let your leaders fear; let the nobles be afraid
All of the world will melt away
The arm of God will hold back the wicked
Let the redeemed of the Lord march on!
The arm of the God will bring the redeemed to Mount Zion
It is the Temple God has made
The Lord will reign from eternity![3]

Amen

The New Song

In 1761 John Wesley placed in a letter to a friend his rules for hymn singing. His goal was to combat the poor singing found in English churches of the time. This was not about singing off key and the like, but abusing the practice of singing to reflect a disordered mess. Wesley condemned the act, believing the songs had become more about the individual and the experience it brought than the divine drama afforded to God.

3. Exodus 15:1–19.

His final rule reads, "Above all, sing spiritually. Have an eye to God in every word you sing. Aim at pleasing Him more than yourself, or any other creature. In order to do this, attend strictly to the sense of what you sing, and see that your heart is not carried away with the sound, but offered to God continually; so shall your singing be such as the Lord will approve of here, and reward when he cometh in the clouds of heaven."[4] There are times we let our religious zeal over take us and our acts of praise become more about ourselves—the moment to experience—than about worshiping God. Even in absolute triumph, we must remember this.

I am somewhat of a hymnal traditionalist. I prefer songs to tell a theological story complete in 5 verses if not more and without a chorus. Further, as many have believed throughout English hymnody, the songs we sing must manifest themselves in our lives. Here in John's liturgy is a song sung in heaven and earth because of God's continual triumph throughout the ages. The song is sung completely and jubilantly even in the midst of the "historical tension."[5]

More, there is the spiritual tune of God and his Creation. St. John of the Cross writes, "But when God visits the soul Himself, the words of the stanza are then true, for, in perfect obscurity, hidden from the enemy, it receives, at such times, the spiritual graces of God."[6] It is this tune we sing in our prayers. It is in this intensely mystical union with God we grasp what real divinity is. He speaks to our soul and our soul to him thusly, keeping in secret those thoughts known only to our spirit (Romans 8.26). "It is a work wrought in obscurity, in the hiding place, wherein the soul is confirmed more and more in union with God by love; and, therefore, the soul sings, 'In darkness and concealment.'"[7] When we reach that heavenly harmonic through our

---

4. These rules were written in 1761, but currently found in the *United Methodist Hymnal*, vii.

5. Ratzinger writes, "Liturgical singing is established in the midst of this great historical tension." He notes the union of Exodus and Revelation as well. See, Ratzinger, *The Spirit of the Liturgy*, 137, along with all of chapter 2.

6. Saint John of the Cross, *The Dark Night of the Soul*, 450–51.

7. Saint John of the Cross, *The Dark Night of the Soul*, 452.

prayers where there is a syncretic relationship, combing human and divine in a *theosis* event, we reach the ultimate contemplative unity.

In the liturgy of the Orthodox Armenian Church, the Trisagion is sung at the beginning of the *Proschume*. "Holy God, Holy and Mighty, Holy and Immortal, who wast crucified for us, have mercy upon us."[8] Following the *Proschume*, clerks and other attendants would sing at various stages.

Perhaps if we sung more during our prayers, or in moments of crisis, we may find a better union with God.

A Prayer of Adoration

> Oh Great God, surround us
> Your wrath is soon to be finished
> Establish us with your people
> Let the angels sing of our redemption
>
> O Great and Marvelous are the works of your hands
> You, Lord God, the Almighty, are Righteous and True
> You alone are king of the nations
> Let us all reverence and glorify your name
>
> O God, you along are holy
> All nations will worship you
> The Heavenly Temple is open
> The righteous of God is revealed
> Grace reigns

---

8. Hammond, *Liturgies: Eastern and Western*, 143.

15

To End God's Wrath

"Then shall the Priest sign himself; and shall request of the true God ... for the forgiveness of his own offenders, enemies, and of those that hate him."[1]

We must approach this chapter with care. This chapter deals with the coming judgment against Babylon, the epitome of the world system. It is the Tower of Babel in Genesis 11, the Babylonians in the rest of the Old Testament, and Rome in the New actively seeking to combat God and His people throughout the ages. As you meditate and pray these prayers imagine you are watching the hailstones fall, the people suffer the wrath of God and hearing the cursing of the sinners. The leader takes this position, while the penitent, or congregation, is the witness.

We are called to consider how the examples of Scripture, such as Job, can serve us in our theological decisions. For instance, can we employ Scripture for help in interceding for those in the world system suffering God's retribution? Scripture is never just one book, but a collection of voices all wrestling with their individual contexts and their own literary families. We cannot take one book out, Revelation, and ignore another, Job. The sores the first angel pours out are similar to the sores Satan inflicts upon Job. Perhaps this is a sign of

1. Hammond, *Liturgies: Eastern and Western*, 164.

God's ultimate testing for his creation? After all, the deal made with Satan was to allow a free hand in dealing with Job, except to take his life, language we find dormant in Revelation.

Or, maybe this has something to do with the plagues God inflicted upon Egypt (Exodus 9:9-11; Deut 28:27). Let's consider that for a moment. Yes, this was because of Egypt's enslavement of the Hebrew people, but like the story in Job, God is ultimately controlling the fate of everyone who has ever lived. Nothing can happen unless God has allowed it. Pharaoh's heart was hardened by God not to punish Egypt, but to provide an example of God's grace. Even with this election, God would not allow Israel to think more highly of themselves than the Egyptians (Amos 9). Other examples are given in Scripture where one group is told not to think themselves above another, even if it looks like the latter group has fallen into God's displeasure (Romans 9–11).

I have often encountered those who would be sorely disappointed if their enemies do not in some way experience hell on earth. Indeed, for them to have Revelation end in any other way but to watch the enemies of God suffer the most horrible of existences would dampen their entry into the Kingdom of God Eternal. It is possible that they do not know Scripture also tells us not to gloat when our enemy falls (Proverbs 24:17).

Remember, as you read these other chapters to prepare for your meditations here, focus on the struggle of life and death in our struggles to forgive our enemies.

The First Prayer: 16:1–6

We hear the mighty voice from the Temple
Go, Angel, pour out the seven vessels of God's wrath
Drown the earth with the wrath of God

We hear the calamity from the city.
We hear a voice from the Temple.
We hear the Lord's voice taking vengeance upon his enemies.

See the first angel leaving the Temple
He pours out God's wrath upon the earth.
O Angel, scar those with the beast's mark
Bring the plague of Job to those who worship the dragon

We rejoice as the Lord pours out his
We praise the Great King who consumes them with his burning anger.[2]

Stand still and watch
The second angel carries the wrath of God to the sea
It becomes as blood and dies
Still yet, the third angel carries the wrath of God
The rivers and the springs die, drowned with blood
O Angel, sing the dirge of God
The Holy One sends these judgments
The wrath of God lays waste those who have persecuted the people of God.
It is their deserved end
For they have devoured your people

We rejoice as the Lord pours out his wrath
O God, save not the nations who rebel against you
O King, destroy those who refuse to acknowledge you
On the kingdoms that do not worship, pour out your wrath
We echo the angel's cry, "It is their just reward."

Amen

Love

G. K. Chesterton in writing about the pride raised by our own ignorance of the virtues we do not possess notes the satisfaction given by comparison. In a rhetorical return to a "priggish little clerk" who supposes himself better than the Mullah (Muslim), Chesterton writes, "'A really good man would be less bloodthirsty than the Mullah. But you are less bloodthirsty, not because you are more of a good

---

2. Psalm 69:24.

man, but because you are a great deal less of a man. You are not bloodthirsty, not because you would spare your enemy, but because you would run away from him."[3] We are not made righteous by comparison to the unrighteous, holy by comparison to the sinner. We are made righteous by the faithfulness of Christ (Romans 3:21–6).

Praying for our enemies with love is perhaps one of the most difficult commandments Jesus has given us, but it was his final example while he was on the cross (Luke 23:34).[4] We should fulfill this example the more so when we see them getting what we believe they are due. After suffering persecution, should we expect people to find it within themselves to pray for those who were just a bit ago laying waste to their friends and families? If we do, can we declare ourselves righteous because we prayed while they preyed?

Ante studium

Hear the angel cry, "They deserve it."

We are not guilty of the sins of our ancestors!
We are in need of compassion, oh Lord.
We are not guilty. Help us, God our Savior.
Help us and glorify your name.
Save and forgive us to honor your name.[5]

The sins of the people were great in the days of Ezekiel
Not even Noah, Daniel, or Job cold have prevented the wrath of God
The sins were so great they could save only themselves[6]

---

3. Chesterton, *All Things Considered*, 48.
4. Roman Catholic Eucharistic theology, as expressed by Dr. Scott Hahn in his book, *Consuming the Word: The New Testament and the Eucharist in the Early Church,* sees the Eucharist as the "sacrifice of the Mass." He draws from this portion of Luke to show how the Passover meal *begins* the sacrifice. This is my theology as well. Therefore, everything happening on the cross is part of the sacrifice enshrined in the Eucharist. If the Eucharist is still ongoing, so is the petition for forgiveness of sins from the Son to the Father.
5. Psalm 79:6–9.
6. Ezekiel 14:20.

> But, O Lord, consider our words
> And consider the salvation of Jesus
> In Jesus the whole world is reconciled to the Father.[7]
>
> **Lord, let us remember Job who offered sacrifices for sin for his children**
> **Remember we who offer sacrifices for sin for others,**
> **This is as Christ is the sacrifice for the world.**
>
> Amen

I place this small prayer in the middle of this chapter to give us pause. Our *ante studium* sets the stage for a major act of this chapter. The people of this world are beginning to suffer under the wrath of God, but the children of God are thought to be safe. We must ask ourselves about our role here. Just as Christ is the mediator between God and man helping to mediate the wrath of God, can we as Christians not mediate the due wrath of God upon our persecutors?

The Second Prayer: Revelation 16:7–12

> Hear now the voices under the altar
> O Lord God, O Almighty One
> Your judgments are true
> Your judgments are just
>
> **O Angel, bring the fourth vessel of God's wrath**
> **Cause the sun to become brighter and burn everyone**
> **But remember us, O Lord**
>
> Stand and see, O people of God, everyone burning by the intense heat
> See them blaspheming the name of God
> They do not repent of their sins
> They do turn to God to give him glory.

---

7. See 2 Corinthian 5:19 and Colossians 1:20.

Lord, let us remember Job who offered sacrifices for sin for his children
Remember we who offer sacrifices for sin for others,
This is as Christ is the sacrifice for the world

Watch as the fifth vessel pours out darkness over the earth
Hear the grinding of teeth as sinners curse God
They are filled with pain and plagues
But they do not turn to repentance

We are your people, but are they?
We are the sheep of your pasture, but are they?
We will always thank you and praise your greatness forever.[8]
Lord, let us remember Job who offered sacrifices for sin for his children
Remember we who offer sacrifices for sin for others,
This is as Christ is the sacrifice for the world

Look and behold, people of God
The Sixth Angel brings out the armies of God
The rivers are dry and they march across them to destroy
They move quickly to kill
This is the wrath of God.

We are your people, but are they?
We are the sheep of your pasture, but are they?
We will always thank you and praise your greatness forever.
Lord, let us remember Job who offered sacrifices for sin for his children
Remember we who offer sacrifices for sin for others,
This is as Christ is the sacrifice for the world
Have we not sinned as well, O Lord?

Amen

---

8. Psalm 79:13.

Forgiveness

This is a difficult section of Scripture. How are we to feel as we see our enemies ready to fall but at the moment suffering under the full weight of God's wrath? We must turn again to the story of the Exodus, when as Egypt began to fall the Israelites turned only to God. They did not gloat but sought comfort in God. I have included a refrain here to prompt the reader to remind God of his promises (Isaiah 43:26).

John intends to remind us we are not always separated from the wrath of God. We too occupy the time and place of those whom we would wish to see disheveled by the divine (Psalm 37; cf. Matthew 5:44–45). To call out to God when we those around us are experiencing severe plight should lead the reader to consider the selfishness of *not* praying for our enemies. What is the harm of praying for our communities, even if we have judged them as worthless? What is more Christ-like? Is it to cheer the wrath of God or to humbly seek the cessation of such an event?

The Third Prayer: Revelation 16:13–21

Stand, the time is near
See the dragon rise and the frogs follow
Behold the terror of the dragon, the beast and the false prophet
They perform false miracles to entice people into rebellion
Rejoice at the end of our enemies

Lord, let us remember Job who offered sacrifices for sin for his children
Remember we who offer sacrifices for sin for others,
This is as Christ is the sacrifice for the world

Hear the voice of the Beloved
Jesus will come quickly to defeat our enemies
If we watch for him, he will save us and will be blessed
He will destroy our enemies as we watch

To End God's Wrath

We recall Israel's journey
Out of God's grace did you feed your people
You gave them quail to feed them in the midst of the desert.
The sinners justly suffered because they tormented your people
They hated he strangers whom you knew as your people.[9]
Lord, let us do good; Lord let us share with others our sacrifices.[10]

Behold the nightmare of the ages has come!
The demons gather the people together to fight our God!
Armageddon, the refrain of all evil and good for ages and ages
But behold, O People of God, hear the voice of God!
It is finished our God proclaims!

But we hear the cry from the cross
We see our savior mocked and thirsty
We give him sour wine with the branch of penance.
On the cross he stayed to say
It is finished
Even now, on the throne he cries
It is finished[11]
It is the cry of forgiveness
It is finished.

Watch the heavens for God's anger
Tremble as the thunder crashes
The sky is broken by thunder, O people of God
The earth shakes, split in two, for the God of Vengeance is awake
See the thunder as it crashes and rolls, and the lightning as it breaks the sky.
It is a great earthquake striking
It is far worse than the world has ever known.

We hear the earthquake, but it not in anger
We remember the earthquake when our savior died
The graves were open and the curtain torn in two
The dead could see the living and the living could see God.[12]

9. Wisdom of Solomon 19:10–13.
10. Hebrews 13:16.
11. John 19:28–30.
12. Matthew 27:51–52.

Alas, O Babylon, or den of sinners, you are destroyed.
We rejoice as the nations fall
God has remembered your sins and pours out his wrath
All the world is not create anew, but without those not worthy

We cry to the Lord!
Open the heavens and come down.
Hurl your lightning and scatter your enemies!
Shoot your arrows and confuse them!
Reach down from heaven and rescue us from the deep waters
From the power of our enemies, redeem us
To you, O God, we will sing a new song!
We will sing of your praises for you grant victory to your King![13]

God rains hail down as sign of his wrath
Still people curse God
Still people do not repent
Let us withhold our prayers from them, O People of God

Lord, let us remember the children of Job.
Let us remember Hymenaeus and Alexander
Remember Onesiphorus who fell away
Remember Paul hopeful refrain.
Remember the words of James, the brother of the Lamb[14]
O God, remember forgiveness and repentance does not cure wrath
Your servant Moses sinned against you, but punished and was redeemed
So, Great God of Mercy, remember now Babylon
We hold them high in our hearts as you are low in their minds
Begin your reign with peace and forgiveness, O God.

Amen

---

13. Psalm 144:5–10.
14. James 5:14–6.

Grace

The other people have sinned. Indeed, they have done many horrible acts against God, Christ, and the Church. They have ridiculed and slaughtered us. They are getting their just reward as the angel cries. This is a scene of awful destruction. As we pray through it, let us remember the imprecatory psalms where the man who is said to be after God's own heart is praying for the deaths of his enemies.

What about our just reward? We have confessed our sins of avarice, greed, false piety, and false witness (see Revelation 2–3). Do we have a just reward still waiting for us?

St. John Chrysostom writes to the people of Antioch to encourage forgiveness of their enemies as God has forgiven them. Should not we then be Christ to the world and absorb the violence their sins are due? In his twentieth homily to the Antiochians, St. John Chrysostom reminds them they should not imagine evil against one another in their heart. He urges us through them to "set aside all wrath; to make the wound disappear." The vengeance we seek for our enemies does nothing but install us as divine torturers. He asks, "If you see a member of your body cut off, won't you do everything your body can to reunite it with your body?"

As we meditate upon the Scriptures, let us consider the people, even our enemies, who are suffering under God's wrath. Can we act as a mediator? Let us also ask ourselves, "What is our just reward?" Is it really Christ? Or do we deserve something dark? Especially when we forget we are nothing without Christ. Let us remain humble and not wish upon our enemies the wrath of God.

In 2 Maccabees 12:38–46, we see one of the most positive affirmations of the resurrection to life before the New Testament. Judah, the mighty hammer of God, wins a victory, but finds many of the fallen had amulets to other gods. He was worried about their souls and offered prayers for them along with a collection to the Temple in their name so that upon the final resurrection they would find forgiveness.

John Wesley, in his 112th sermon writes,

> "And in hell he lifted up his eyes."—O, what a change! How is the mighty fallen! But the word which is here rendered hell does not always mean the place of the damned. It is, literally, the invisible world; and is of very wide extent, including the receptacle of separate spirits, whether good or bad. But here it evidently means, that region of hades where the souls of wicked men reside, as appears from the following words, "Being in torment;"—"in order," say some, "to atone for the sins committed while in the body, as well as to purify the soul from all its inherent sin." Just so, the eminent heathen poet, near two thousand years ago:—
>
> ....
>
> See the near resemblance between the ancient and the modern purgatory! Only in the ancient, the heathen purgatory, both fire, water, and air, were employed in expiating sin, and purifying the soul; whereas in the mystic purgatory, fire alone is supposed sufficient both to purge and expiate. Vain hope! No suffering, but that of Christ, has any power to expiate sin; and no fire, but that of love, can purify the soul, either in time or in eternity.[15]

Did Wesley believe in what we understand as Purgatory? Doubtful, as he has many statements against "Romish purgatory," however, he does express a hope for a refinement through Christ during the intermediate state between death and the new life.[16]

St. John of the Cross writes regarding purgatory,

> In the third place we learn incidentally how souls suffer in Purgatory. The fire would have no power over them if they were perfectly prepared for the kingdom of God, and union with Him in glory, and if they had no faults to expiate, which are the matter on which that fire seizes; for

---

15. Wesley, *Sermons*, Sermon 112.

16. For a deeper discussion on purgatory from a Protestant standpoint, and how modern Protestants may recapture something of an ancient model, see Walls, *Purgatory: The Logic of Total Transformation*.

when that matter is consumed there is nothing more to burn. So is it here, when all imperfections are removed, the suffering of the soul ceases, and in its place comes joy as deep as it is possible for it to be in this life.

In the fourth place, we learn that the soul, the more it is purified and cleansed in the fire of love, the more it glows with it. The more the fuel is prepared for the fire the more it burns; though the soul is not always conscious of this burning of love within it, but only now and then, when the ray of contemplation shines upon it not so strongly. Then the soul is enabled to see, and even to enjoy, the work that is going on; it seems as if the hand of the artificer was withdrawn from the work, and the iron taken out of the furnace, so as to show in some measure the work that is being wrought. Then, too, the soul may see in itself that good which it could not see while the process was going on. Thus, when the flame ceases to envelope the fuel it burns, we see clearly how much of it has been enkindled.[17]

C. S. Lewis writes,

> I believe in Purgatory. Mind you, the Reformers had good reasons for throwing doubt on the "Romish doctrine concerning Purgatory" as that Romish doctrine had then become...
>
> Religion has claimed Purgatory. Our souls demand Purgatory, don't they? Would it not break the heart if God said to us, "It is true, my son, that your breath smells and your rags drip with mud and slime, but we are charitable here and no one will upbraid you with these things, nor draw away from you. Enter into the joy?" Should we not reply, "With submission, sir, and if there is no objection, I'd rather be cleaned first." "It may hurt, you know"—"Even so, sir."
>
> I assume that the process of purification will normally involve suffering. Partly from tradition; partly because most

---

17. Saint John of the Cross, *The Dark Night of the Soul*, 403–4.

> real good that has been done me in this life has involved it. But I don't think the suffering is the purpose of the purgation . . .
>
> My favourite image on this matter comes from the dentist's chair. I hope that when the tooth of life is drawn and I am "coming round," a voice will say, "Rinse your mouth out with this." This will be Purgatory. The rinsing may take longer than I can now imagine. The taste of this may be more fiery and astringent than my present sensibility could endure. But . . . it will [not] be disgusting and unhallowed.[18]

Throughout Scripture we are given the command to pray for our enemies as a continual decree without a given end, mirroring the petition of Christ in Luke 23:34. Are we to think their death includes the end of this commandment? Let the direction of your prayer be like that of Paul in 2 Timothy 1:16–18. Pray for your enemies, even if they have left our world. Pray as well for the saints who have fallen. Pray that all those in the waterless pit return to God and God's ultimate freedom (Zechariah 9:11).

Let the focus of our prayers be like the anaphora found in the Ethiopic Church,

> For prisoners we beseech, that the Lord loose them from their bonds
>
> For captives we beseech, that the Lord restore them to their country in peace
>
> For those of the Christian congregation who are fallen asleep we beseech, that the Lord vouchsafe them a place of rest
>
> For the sick and suffering we beseech, that the Lord heal them speedily and send upon them loving-kindness and mercy

---

18. Lewis, *Letters to Malcolm Chiefly on Prayer*, 108–9.

For those of our fathers and our brothers and our sisters who have trespassed we beseech, that the Lord cherish not anger against them but grant them rest and relief from his wrath.[19]

After each petition, the congregation was to say, "Lord have mercy upon us." We note the petitions for the prisoners, the captives, those already asleep and those who are fallen into sin. Perhaps we may be so humble as to pray this way.

Lord, have mercy upon us.

A Prayer of Intercession

O Angels of God, bring out the wrath of God
Barachiel, you bring plagues to the people if they worship the dragon
Gabriel, bring to us the death of the sea
Murder the rivers and the springs, Raphael
Let the waters become like blood

You, O God, are righteous in your judgments
For the blood of the saints has long watered the earth
Do not now the sinners deserve the same?
Oh My Jesus, will you punish the wicked like this?

Uriel, O Angel of the Sun, scorch the sinners with intense light
O Lord, is this really the light of the Gospel?
Are not all sinners like Job, burning in the refiner's fire?
Do those in the fire still not repent?
O Lord, their cursing continues

Simiel, as Uriel brought light, bring now darkness and pain
Let them still yet blaspheme God in their pain
O My Jesus, the people still do not repent
Let Oriphiel bring the armies of wrath across the river
O My Jesus, will you not stop this?

---

19. Brightman, *Liturgies: Eastern and Western*, 208.

Praying in God's Theater

Dear God, we tremble at the refrain of Armageddon
For years, everything is Armageddon
We tell our children Armageddon
Jesus, in all of your power cannot you not stop it?
O Lord, Lamb for Sinners Slain, does Armageddon slay the Gospel?

Jesus, we see the armies gathering against
We are awake and see this
O Lord, send Michael with your voice
Shout, It is Finished!
Let the cry from the cross me the final words to the wicked
Let all flesh be reconciled to God
It is finished!

Let the skies fall and the earth shake
Let the might be humbled
O Lord, you are the same who on the cross, thirsty and tired
It is finished!
Bring an end to our rebellion, O Lord
Cool now the refiner's fire
Salt us and purge us of our sins
Join now salvation with the call,
It is finished!

16

Prayers of Confession

"By the Rivers of Babylon, there we wept."[1]

In the last chapter we used Job as a model of prayer. He, after all, prayed in the absence of his children and was heralded by God for such an action. We may examine Moses as well who stood between God and Israel to prevent their destruction (Exodus 32; cf., Psalm 106:23). Nehemiah is also a captain of our faith in praying for those who were standing against him.

In the New Testament we have two examples from the Apostle Paul who, finding others in sin, grieved in himself and sought their rectification. In 2 Corinthians 11:28–29, we read,

> Apart from these external things, there is the responsibility that weighs on me every day, my anxious concern for all the churches. [29] Is anyone weak? I share his weakness. If anyone brings about the downfall of another, does my heart not burn with anger? If boasting there must be, I will boast of the things that show up my weakness.

In Colossians 1.24, Paul writes, "It is now my joy to suffer for you; for the sake of Christ's body, the church, I am completing what

---

1. Psalm 137.1

still remains for Christ to suffer in my own person." Perhaps Paul has in mind the words of Jesus in John 14:12, "In very truth I tell you, whoever has faith in me will do what I am doing; indeed he will do greater things still because I am going to the Father." As Thomas Aquinas would later state, Christ and the Church are one mystical person, with Christ as the head. Thus, Paul is fulfilling the measure of Christ by absorbing the sufferings needed to continue the perfection of the Church.

We are left with example after example of this tension between reality and perfection. Christ has suffered once for all, providing justification for all, and now commands us to continue his life through our own as the Church. It is not that the work of Christ is in deficit, but that we become Christ to the world, so that we take up the prayers he uttered and the sufferings he endured.

We, to participate in the union afforded by Christ, must become the lost, the rebellious Babylon so that we may through our prayers seek their and our perfection.

The First Prayer: Revelation 17:1–13

O Lord, our empires stretch over the earth
We conquer all
Abusing all in unnatural ways
Judge us, Great God

We are a greedy people and have sold the gospel
We are drunk on power
We lust after what others have craving only more
We have become like Rome of Old

Our empire lies in ruin
But still we grow, like cancer with never enough
We are the sickness in the world
We are no longer salt, but sin.

From us spring forth other sicknesses and other devourers.
We have brought about abominations

We lead others astray with our gold
It is we who have murdered your people, even ourselves
Tell no one of our sins, O Lord

We ascend from the pit to bring destruction
We wage war against all, O Lord
It is us who has summoned the dragon
We have given the beast its power!

We wage war against the Lamb by our sin
But he will overcome us
He is the Lord of Lords and King of Kings!
His people are called the chosen and faithful!

O God, like Egypt and Judas, you have put into our hearts rebellion
Do we not fulfill your purpose?
Do we not seek to do your words?
Purge us now, Great King, our sins by your fire

Amen

We Are the Beast

When John first wrote this, Rome followed in the line of Babylon, Edom, and Assyria as the spiritual darkness oppressing God's people. Lately, those who hold to a dispensationalist viewpoint of Revelation have begun to list various geopolitical entities as this "Rome." Often times the Roman Catholic Church is targeted as the unholy evil. No doubt imperial Rome is in view here in John's historical setting but to set the posture of this chapter I want you to consider yourself as the beast, the dragon, and the oppressor. Consider how we as the Church may have erred during the dominance of what is labeled Christendom.

There are two apologies (defenses) from the second century directed to Caesar. The first is from an unknown author and entitled the Epistle to Diognetus. A rather well known Christian theologian, Justin Martyr, writes the second. Both argue for recognition by Rome of Christianity. They argue not for some cultural superiority, or the need to have Christianity declared the only State religion. Rather, they argue for a culturally pacifist Christianity, maintaining its own truth, but not denying to anyone some measure of the Logos.

In one part of the Epistle to Diognetus, there is a striking list of virtues enumerated by the apologist. We read,

> But, inhabiting Greek as well as barbarian cities, according as the lot of each of them has determined, and following the customs of the natives in respect to clothing, food, and the rest of their ordinary conduct, they display to us their wonderful and confessedly striking method of life. They dwell in their own countries, but simply as sojourners. As citizens, they share in all things with others, and yet endure all things as if foreigners. Every foreign land is to them as their native country, and every land of their birth as a land of strangers. They marry, as do all [others]; they beget children; but they do not destroy their offspring. They have a common table, but not a common bed. They are in the flesh, but they do not live after the flesh. They pass their days on earth, but they are citizens of heaven. They obey the prescribed laws, and at the same time surpass the laws by their lives. They love all men, and are persecuted by all. They are unknown and condemned; they are put to death, and restored to life. They are poor, yet make many rich; they are in lack of all things, and yet abound in all; they are dishonoured, and yet in their very dishonour are glorified. They are evil spoken of, and yet are justified; they are reviled, and bless; they are insulted, and repay the insult with honour; they do good, yet are punished as evil-doers. When punished, they rejoice as if quickened into life; they are assailed by the Jews as foreigners, and are persecuted by the Greeks; yet those who hate them are unable to assign any reason for their hatred.[2]

---

2. *Diognetus* 5 in *ANF,* 1:126–27.

Prayers of Confession

Is this our Christianity today? Are we these things or have we in many ways become the Roman Empire, Edom, Assyria, and Babylon? Perhaps this is why we hear calls for the downfall of Christendom in the West—not from without, but within, so we may once again reclaim the position of the loyal opposition where we stand against the powers when it is needful and warranted so that we are seen as the other, the kingdom of God rather than a kingdom of mere men and women.

If you are so inclined, examine for yourself modern Western Christianity next to the description of Babylon in Revelation 17 and Babylon's sins in Revelation 18. We have come close to what John warns us against.

The Second Prayer: Revelation 18:1–24

O My Jesus, declare to us that our empire is fallen
Fallen is our empire of individuality
Gone are those walls we have built to keep you out
Cleanse the unclean spirits dwelling in our hearts

We have become drunk on immorality
Our filth is spread among the nations
We have made the merchants of rebellion rich
Still yet you call to us to come

Our sins are like Babel, reaching to heaven
Remember, Great God, our wickedness
Give back to us the rebellions we have caused against you
Repay our evilness with more
Great God, King of Heaven, give to us what we deserve
Where we have stolen your glory to use as our lust, give us suffering
For we have placed ourselves as the Queen of Heaven
Our eyes desire to see only ourselves
Destroy us in our selfishness

Draw us a dirge, O people, lament for us
Weep for us those we've made rich with our sins

> Weep, merchants, for your spring is dry
> Sing to us woes while our empire falls
> O Lord, your judgment is upon us.
> Free those we have enslaved
> Strip us naked of the clothes we have stolen
> O God, lay waste to our land
> Like Jerusalem of old, salt our soil
>
> Jesus, Jesus, we are laid waste before you
> Let the heavens rejoice and the saints sing for joy
> The evils we have done are now returning to us
> You have announced your judgment against us
> Rise against us, O Lord, and judge us for our rebellion against you
> Throw us into the waters and drown us in our sins
> For it is we who have killed your prophets
>
> Amen

Our Sins Before the World

The prayer of confession is a well-worn method of public displays of penitence. We find it throughout Scripture, especially in the Psalms, as well as other Jewish literature common in the Second Temple period, such as Baruch 1:15—3:8. It is in Psalm 51 we find a heart-wrenching example when David confesses his sin for all time before God and the world. In many of our churches, we will find some sort of corporative prayer of confession. It is in this time we submit ourselves to examination.

Yet, I wonder if these well-written and rehearsed prayers are not acting in a detrimental way to our own spirituality. There is nothing wrong—rather, more right than not—in including prayers of confession as a litany on Sunday morning; however, if we do not internalize what the liturgist has crafted out of the bosom of her heart, then they remain words set before us.

The prayer of confession is meant to draw us into union with God in several ways. First, we confess our sins publicly. Second, we

Prayers of Confession

confess and seek repentance for the sins of our neighbors. We are not allowed to progress in the Christian faith alone. In the Christian faith, we are bound to the Holy Trinity, the eternal community of Father, Son, and Holy Spirit existing in a perichoretic unity. The Church is a building of saints, together and not individually (1 Corinthians 12:14, among others). The Church and Christ are one. We are responsible for one another (Matthew 18:15). Thus, the prayer of confession, joining us to one another and requiring we take upon ourselves the sins of others in confession, is an essential element to the community because it binds us together.

The act of the prayer of confession was enshrined early in Christian doctrine. Canon II of the Synod of Laodicea (held between 343 and 381) reads, "Sinners of various kinds who have persevered in the prayer of confession and penance and who have completely turned away from evil shall, after a time of penance that is proportionate to the seriousness of their sins, be again received into communion due to the mercy and goodness of God."[3]

St. Bonaventure gave specific instructions for this, writing "We should know that, in prayer, there are three steps or stages: first, we deplore our misery, then we implore God's mercy, and, finally, we worship him. For we cannot worship God unless we have first obtained grace from Him, nor can we induce God's mercy to confer this grace upon us unless we first grieve for and confess our wretchedness."[4]

In the Nestorian liturgy, we find mention of a mediatory prayer. "Let us all confess and make request and beseech the Lord in purity and groaning. Stand ye fairly and behold those things that are done in the fearful mysteries which are being hallowed. The priest hath drawn nigh to pray that by his mediation peace may be multiplied

---

3. Johnson, *Worship in the Early Church: An Anthology of Historical Sources*, Vol. 2, 299.

4. Saint Bonaventure, "Mystical Opuscula," 73.

unto you. Cast down your eyes and stretch forth your thoughts to heaven."[5]

How dangerous might it be if we, instead of applying to our enemies the label of *boemand*, real or fictitious, we take it upon ourselves to seek the intercession for their sins as if they were our own?

---

5. Brightman, *Liturgies: Eastern and Western*, 282.

17

The Table of the Lord

> "But above all, the time of Christ's last coming, is that of the consummation of the church's marriage with the Lamb, and of the complete and most perfect joy of the wedding."[1]

Our time in the "theatre of reception" draws to a close. In doing so, we are invited into the inner sanctum of the union between God and his creation. Throughout the Gospels we are met with the image of the bride and the bridegroom, an image representing the union between Jesus and the Church just as the Incarnation conjoins God and humanity. In Ephesians, the mystery is made known that we are the bride. It is here we are to meet our bridegroom and enjoy the wedding banquet.

This imagery is not new; it is the same imagery found in Jeremiah or one of the prophets regarding God and His people. It is secured by the rabbinical prohibition against interpreting the *Song of Solomon* in any way but allegorically representing God and Israel. Christians later enshrined this technique as well, but it is now Christ and the Church. While our depraved minds may seek to make light of this image in a rather vulgar and unbecoming way, it is the image

---

1. Edwards, *The Works of Jonathan Edwards, Vol. 2*, 22.

selected by the Apostles and Prophets to present to us the close union of God and the His people through Jesus. Instead of innuendo usually accompanying such talk, we must begin with the first command of marriage in Genesis 2:24:

> That is why a mean leaves his father and mother and attaches himself to his wife, and the two become one.

In this singular verse, we understand the ideal of marriage as given by God. It is not about lordship and the obliteration of (female) identity, but about a union so deep there is simply just one being. Note the direction of attachment. The man leaves his father and mother to attach himself to his wife. The union is not about absorbing the female into the male, but about the male seeking the female to attach himself to her.

This is the story of Incarnation—of Jesus and the Church. In several parables, the image is drawn of a man traveling into a foreign country to look for something. In reality, we know Christ left the heavens to seek out a covenantal people in much the same way Isaac sought Rebekah. The dutiful son, leaving the nurturing attachment springing from the natural bond, travels to find his wife. Their bond is meant to be deeper because it is a spiritual bond.

This bond is achieved with Christ. We have been justified by his acts and by nothing we have done. However, while we are in the process of salvation, we will continue to affirm and in confirmation we renew our union with Christ. We do this by the communication of grace through the sacraments, two of which are held in common by all streams of Christianity. In baptism, we begin our union with Christ. At the Table of the Lord we meet in communion with one another and with Christ in certain unity to receive medicine for our souls, to reaffirm our Christian walk, and to meet Jesus in the most humanly way possible. The Eucharist becomes our personal relationship with Jesus.

Between baptism and the celebration of our unity we seek to encounter God in a rather spiritual way, through prayer. During our contemplative unity, we seek to grasp the mystical presence of Jesus through the power of the groaning of the Holy Spirit. We are pulled deeper to God as we remove ourselves from our prayers. Our prayers, as we proceed with contemplative unity with Christ, become our praxis for what we will celebrate when we partake of certain unity of the Eucharist.

Contemplating unity is not the same as certain unity. We can only encounter God through our prayers in a transcendent manner. Contemplating the Eucharist is as effective as contemplating the Christian life, however. To invest ourselves in taking the mind's journey into what we may expect to find begins to transform us, slowly and surely. To begin to decide if the journey is one we want to experience forces us to grapple with what we are in the light of the reality of God. In contemplating the Eucharist, we must understand that nothing can render to us the medicine for our souls the mere bread and wine does. Likewise, in Eucharistic contemplation, we begin to surrender ourselves to the mystery of the real presence and remember just how ill we really are, but because of God the Son we are made whole.

The First Prayer: Revelation 19:1–10

Hear the Hallelujahs
Salvation! Glory! Power! belong to our God
Hear the voices from heaven sing praises
The judgments of the Lord are true and righteous
Babylon is judged.
The blood of the saints are remembered

We do not deserve the Lord's grace
We glorify the name of the Lord
In his mercy he is faithful
When others laugh
When others say, where is your God
Our God reigns in heaven

Sing Hallelujah
Babylon's ash rises to the heavens
Let the throne's chorus sing Amen
Let the angels sing Hallelujah
Obey the command from the throne
Let us give God our praise,
We who fear the Lord, stature matters not
Let us give God our praise
Sing Hallelujah
Our God reigns

Let the house of Israel fear the Lord
Let the house of Aaron fear the Lord
Let all of us fear the Lord
He is our help and our shield
O Lord, remember us and bless us
Our God will bless those who fear him, stature matters not[2]

Rejoice! Be glad! Give the glory to God!
The Marriage of the Lamb is here! We are ready, O Lord
Let us adorn ourselves in white, for our works makes us righteous
We are blessed; the Lord invites us
These are the true words of God!

O God of Zion, we owe our hymn of praise
Let us fulfill our vows to you
O Lord, hear our prayers
Our flesh continues with our wicked works
We are overcome in our sins
Only you can pardon us, O God
We are blessed to be brought into your courts
Let us be the good things of your house, your Temple

The angels are our follow servants
They too hold the witness of Jesus Christ
They too worship God
The witness of Jesus is this prophecy

---

2. Psalm 115:1–18.

Your justice, O Lord, answers our sins
O God our savior, redeem us
You are the hope of all the earth
You are clothed in power
You have created this world by your might
Redeem us and it, O God[3]

Amen

Hallelujah

This is the only section in Revelation to mention the word hallelujah. It comes from the *Hallel* Psalms. Psalms 111–18 follow immediate the context of 108–10 where the ancient compiler of the psalms placed the songs dedicated to the coming king. "These psalms function as praise for the coming and triumph of the messiah" found just before.[4] No wonder the hallelujahs were shouted.

The jubilation of taking the Eucharist is often described in a manifold of ways, with a plethora of words failing to suffice. F. Thomas, in *Leggenda Minore*, writes of the mystic St. Catherine of Siena:

> Sometimes she saw the holy angels serving around the altar at which the Mass was celebrated, holding in their hands a golden veil, or in company with the saints, praising and blessing God. Sometimes she saw three Faces in one substance, or the altar and the priest wrapt in a flame of fire. At other times a great and marvellous splendour seemed to shine forth from the altar; or again, when the priest divided the sacred Host, it was manifestly shown how all was in each part; and often she beheld the Holy Trinity under various appearances and signs. Sometimes the sacred Host was transformed into the likeness of Jesus Christ Himself, at various ages, or she beheld It consecrated under the appearances of fire, flesh, or blood. Often also she saw above the altar the Queen of Heaven who reverently adored the

---

3. Psalm 65:1–8.
4. Barber, *Coming Soon*, 226.

Blessed Sacrament; besides which, on many occasions, she discerned a consecrated from an unconsecrated Host.[5]

St. Gregory of Nazianzus writes,

> Now we will partake of a Passover which is still typical; though it is plainer than the old one. For that is ever new which is now becoming known. It is ours to learn what is that drinking and that enjoyment, and His to teach and communicate the Word to His disciples. For teaching is food, even to the Giver of food. Come hither then, and let us partake of the Law, but in a Gospel manner, not a literal one; perfectly, not imperfectly; eternally, not temporarily. Let us make our Head, not the earthly Jerusalem, but the heavenly City; not that which is now trodden under foot by armies, but that which is glorified by Angels. Let us sacrifice not young calves, nor lambs that put forth horns and hoofs, in which many parts are destitute of life and feeling; but let us sacrifice to God the sacrifice of praise upon the heavenly Altar, with the heavenly dances; let us hold aside the first veil; let us approach the second, and look into the Holy of Holies. Shall I say that which is a greater thing yet? Let us sacrifice *ourselves* to God; or rather let us go on sacrificing throughout every day and at every moment. Let us accept anything for the Word's sake. By sufferings let us imitate His Passion: by our blood let us reverence His Blood: let us gladly mount upon the Cross. Sweet are the nails, though they be very painful. For to suffer with Christ and for Christ is better than a life of ease with others.[6]

The breadth of joyous reception of the Eucharist is found in our ancient liturgies as well. Indeed, the entire liturgy is not designed around a homiletic effort of the minister, or some sermon given according to the daily lectionary; it is not designed towards or for the Eucharist; the ancient liturgy springs *from* the celebration of the

---

5. Drane, *The History of St. Catherine of Siena and Her Companions*, Vol. 2, 39–40.

6. St. Gregory Nazianzen, "Select Orations," (*NPNF* 7:431).

Eucharist. Such a theological move is found in the earliest Christian liturgical dramas including the first century Didache.

It would be surprising *not* to see the Eucharist at this point in John's work. After all, if we follow something of the structure laid out in the Psalms (shown aptly by Barber as noted above) and Paul's statement beginning with 1 Corinthians 11:26, the Eucharist is both the antecedent to and consequence of Christ. It is given to commemorate his death and to look forward to his coming. This we do to memorialize Jesus, but this is not simply a part of the human memory. This is the same memory assigned to the Jewish Passover. It is the everlasting and effectual memory transforming with each remembrance. Equally it is understood as the bridge like Jacob's ladder between heaven and earth. If we are to fully join with Christ, symbolized by the wedding, then it is to occur at the Eucharist.

So many look to the skies to await the return of Jesus. In our current times, people write of Syria or Russia to measure them against ancient empires and peoples, believing Jesus is soon to return. With each national, or even individual, tragedy, Jesus is said to simply wait in the clouds, just beyond our vision, to return and end this maddening mess. Christians become exhausted, tired, and weary waiting year and year, generation after generation for Jesus to return.

Many Christians believe the return of Jesus spoken of in Paul's letters and in the Gospels has already occurred and thus we are to continue with our Christian journey, intent on saving souls from hell, while believing we will go on forever, waiting to meet Christ when we die. They become exhausted, tired, and weary with no hope except to die and then meet Jesus.

Both are equally wrong.

Both are somewhat right.

We must continue to look for the coming of Jesus, understanding the Second Coming spoken of in the New Testament has already occurred; however, we are given bipartite commands in Scripture. While Christ has physically returned during the destruction of the Temple, he now spiritually returns in the Eucharist. John 6.52–58 gives the final summation of the Eucharist. It is to give us eternal life. We are not told to take it once, but to continue to take it. It does not simply act as a remembrance of a singular event but serves as the medicine for our souls, giving us life eternal. This is the certain unity, the moment we are truly unified with Christ.

The Second Prayer: Revelation 19:11–21

Behold a second door in heaven
See the rider of the white horse
He judges and wars; his name is faithful and true
Only he knows his name
His eyes are fire and his head crowned

We will clap our hands
Let us shout to God with joy
We fear the Lord Most High
O Lord, you are the Great King
We are subject to you![7]

His robe is dipped in blood
Let us call his name the Word of God
Behold the armies of heaven, the saints above us
Clothed in righteousness, they follow him
His tongue is a sharp sword
Behold him as he strikes down the nations
He will rule them with a rod of iron
The grapes of wrath are trodden by his feet
He is the wrath of God.
He is our King of Kings and Lord of Lords

O Lord, wield the sword with mercy
You are a mighty warrior
Ride out in majesty
Ride out to seek truth, humility, and justice
Let your right hand show your good works

---

7. Psalm 47:2–4.

The nations will cower before you
Your enemies will suffer shame
Your throne, O God, stands always
Your rod is one of justice
O Lamb, you are anointed above all kings[8]

Behold the angel standing on the sun
Come, he shouts, assemble!
Let the birds of the air devour the destruction of the earth
For our sinful flesh is defeated
Let it return to the corruption that birthed it
Let stature fall before God

Judge us, O God
Give justice to the children of Adam
We have committed crimes against you
We have brought violence to your creation
We have been corrupt since birth
There is a reward for the just, O Lord
There is a God who is our judge.[9]

Behold the beast and kings of the earth stand to fight
O Lord, seize your enemies and through them into the Lake of Fire
Let those who worship the beast still find their way there.

Our God will destroy the beast's fangs
He will cause the kings of the earth to vanish
He will trod them under like the grass of the field
We will rejoice to see this day
We will bathe in the justice of the wicked
God is our judge[10]

Amen

---

8. Psalm 45:3–8.
9. Psalm 58:2–4, 12.
10. Psalm 58:7–12.

Absorbing the Violent Sword

I want to return to the posture of absorbing violence as we did in chapter 15. I suggest we follow the model of atonement wherein we see Christ taking upon himself the sins of the world (Matthew 8:17; John 1:29; 2 Corinthians 12:10). In doing so, we understand more assuredly what it means to pray in intercession for those around us. We do not need to force others to follow Christ, but act in such a way as to absorb, and correct, what evils they perpetuate. This is not a novel position. Rather, it is one based in the ancient theology of St. Irenaeus.

> And since the apostasy tyrannized over us unjustly, and, though we were by nature the property of the omnipotent God, alienated us contrary to nature, rendering us its own disciples, the Word of God, powerful in all things, and not defective with regard to His own justice, did righteously turn against that apostasy, and redeem from it His own property, not by violent means, as the [apostasy] had obtained dominion over us at the beginning, when it insatiably snatched away what was not its own, but by means of persuasion, as became a God of counsel, who does not use violent means to obtain what He desires; so that neither should justice be infringed upon, nor the ancient handiwork of God go to destruction. Since the Lord thus has redeemed us through His own blood, giving His soul for our souls, and His flesh for our flesh, and has also poured out the Spirit of the Father for the union and communion of God and man, imparting indeed God to men by means of the Spirit, and, on the other hand, attaching man to God by His own incarnation, and bestowing upon us at His coming immortality durably and truly, by means of communion with God,—all the doctrines of the heretics fall to ruin.[11]

---

11. St. Irenaeus, *Against Heresies*, in *ANF,* 1:527.

St. Irenaeus is writing of the atonement, usually pictured in violent terms and derided by some as child abuse. This is not the case and as we often do with our too-human minds, we destroy the beauty of the divine image with the corruption of our own. Instead of giving us over to our own sins, the Holy Trinity absorbed our sins, corrected our spirit and placed us back into the will of God. Our salvation is not based *on* force (determinism) or coercion (threats of hell), but *in* God in Christ who has absorbed all things into himself through the act of reconciliation upon the Cross. God did not issue wrath, but in surrendering to it, overcame it.

Is this a weakness? St. Gregory of Nyssa writes, "Amongst our notions of God no disposition tending to weakness goes along with our belief in Him. We do not say that a physician is in weakness when he is employed in healing one who is so. For though he touches the infirmity he is himself unaffected by it."[12] Oddly enough, we now treat many diseases with weakened forms of the deadly illness, which injected into the body produces antibodies. Our bodies absorb these weakened violent offenders to ward off the living death.

"In countering the Deceiver's unjust rule over humanity due to his apostasy and rebellion, God chose a just way, recovering what was his own not through coercion or by arbitrary fiat, but by way of persuasion, as was fitting to the character of God. God would redeem humanity not by force, but by taking responsibility for us, allowing the Enemy to stumble over his own follies."[13] We are not healed in body by force or redeemed by force, but because God has absorbed the violence, we are made his. This then, is not due to our actions, but the actions of the holy other—of God.

I write this to point us towards the goal of taking within ourselves the condemnations found in Revelation. We are eager always to take the blessings and to give the condemnation; however, we do not consider how we might absorb this for others, following the

---

12. St. Gregory of Nyssa, *The Great Catechism*, (*NPNF* 5:488).
13. Oden, *The Word of Life: Systematic Theology*, Vol. II, 397.

image God gave us within himself. Might we again turn to Job and to his saintly example?

When we read these passages where the enemies of God's people are slaughtered, should we rejoice? Perhaps we would understand better God's salvation and our place in it if we took their sins and their fate upon ourselves, if even in prayer. Just as God became human to take away the violence due us, we should endeavor to take upon ourselves the condemnation afforded sinners, lest we find ourselves surprised at their fate and ours.

A Prayer of Adoration

> O God, You have given us your salvation
> You have avenged our blood
> You have heard our prayers
>
> We give praise to you, O Great God
> For the Lord God Almighty reigns forever!
>
> We will rejoice and give the Son Glory
> We will rejoice at our union
> Clothe us O Lord in our deeds
> Let us eat at your table.
>
> On your table, let the skies open O Lord
> Judge us and defeat our sins
> Give us your words; right our wrongs
> Strike out our wickedness.
>
> Let us eat the body and the blood, the bread and the wine
> Let us commune with you, O Holy Trinity
> Bind us in this moment
> Defeat our sins
> Defeat the beast and the dragon
>
> Amen.

18

A Homily—The Eucharistic Vision

"Blessed be the God of Israel, the one who keeps mercy for his covenant and pledges of deliverance for the people he has redeemed."[1]

Revelation 20 and 21 are better positioned as vision elaborating the benefits of the Eucharist. I propose to see it as a homiletic recounting of the new reality presented in the imparting of the heavenly meal. There is the chaining of the dragon and his eventual defeat. The "little while" may come to symbolize either the weekly fast between celebrations, the moments between prayer, or the length of time between hoping and the fulfillment of that hope (i.e., from certain unity (taking the Eucharist) to ultimate unity, or life eternal). There is life again in these chapters. The martyrs for Jesus find life (20:4) as we are reminded in the death of Christ all are made alive. John writes of judgment (20:11–15), a reality that must accompany the taking of the Eucharist (2 Corinthians 11:28–32. With this, there is death as well.

Revelation 21:2 tells us of the Heavenly Jerusalem, bringing to earth the throne of God and the Lamb. It is not we who go to heaven,

---

1. 4Q491 in Martinez and Tigchelaar, *The Dead Sea Scrolls Study Edition*, 135.

but heaven that comes to us. This is the dialogic communication of grace the Eucharist presents. When this happens, we are united with God. Our contemplation and our hope are given away to the ultimate reality. We are with God and God is with us! Further, all things are made new—anew; renewed. It is another simply another life, but a life completely transformed.

Equally so, even with the condemnations present, there is a hope for those outside the city. While in 21:8, we are told there is no hope for those outside the city, it is in 21:24 we are told those outside—the hopeless and defeated sinners—will come *inside* the city to worship our God. This is the hopeful promise of the Eucharist that we may all share in the suffering of Christ so that we may all share in the life of Christ.

The First Prayer: Revelation 20:1–15

We pray, O Lord, for the angel with the keys and the chain
To bind forever the dragon, the devil, Satan
Throw him into the pit, shut and seal it
Let him deceive the nations no longer
Let us have peace until he must be defeated

O Lord, you are our refuge always
Before the world was created, from forever to forever,
You are our God
If we return to the dust, you are our God
A thousand years is nothing in your eyes
You are our God

Let us see the thrones of judgment, Our God
We see the souls who bore witness to your life in their death
They did not worship the dragon but were marked for you
O Lord, let them reign with you forever and ever

O Lord, we are overcome in your anger
Your have kept our sins before you
In the light of your face, all is made known

A Homily—The Eucharistic Vision

Our life is nothing before your wrath
We are granted by a short space here
Our days pass like vapor
Teach us, O Lord, to use our days wisely
Let us gain your wisdom

O God, when your time has come
Let the dead rise; this is the first resurrection
Those who are dead are blessed and holy
Death no longer has power over them
They will reign with God and Christ forever and ever

O God, give us peace!
Give us mercy in the morning
Let our days be for joy
You have humbled us with trials
But show your servants your works
Show your glory to your children!
May the Grace of the Lord and God be ours
Sanctify the works of our hands, O Lord![2]

O Lord, release the dragon
Let him deceive the nations for just a little longer
Let the princes of the past gather for way
Our enemies believe they number like the sand
Our enemies surround us and the holy city
Let your fire consume them
But, O Lord, let only the beast and the false prophet suffer

God, our God, save us from the waters of chaos!
We have sunk into the deep, into despair
We are overwhelmed and we cry out
Our eyes look for God, but cannot see him
Our enemies out number us.
O God, you know our faults
Let us wait for you, God of Heaven's Armies
Let us seek you, O God of Israel
Let us honor you with our praise

2. Psalm 90:1–17.

Praying in God's Theater

**Bear no insult on account of us, O Lord
Let us Pray to you, O Lord**[3]

We behold the great white throne and the one who sits there
From your presence, O God, all wickedness flees
We behold the dead of all stature before the throne
Let the books be opened
Let us be judged
Let us be found in the Book of Life
Will our works be judged acceptable, O God?

**We pray to you, O Lord
Grant us your grace
Answer us with deliverance
Pull us from the pit
Save us, O Lord; do not let us drown
Answer us with your abundant love
Turn to us with your great mercy
Come, O God, redeem our life**[4]

Let the sea give up the dead
Let the grave give up the dead
Let all be judged according to their works!
O God, throw the sea and the grave into the lake of fire
This is the second death!
Let all those who are in the Book of Life rejoice for death is defeated!

**God will rescue his city!
He will rebuild this land
We will live here and it will be ours
Let those who love the name of God live here always**[5]

Amen

---

3. Psalm 69:1–4, 6–7, 14.
4. Psalm 69:14–19.
5. Psalm 69:36–7.

The End of War

When St. Antony the Great decided to lead the ascetic life, he retreated to the desert. He promptly meets the devil intending to tempt the monk away from the path to a deeper life in God. His fourth century biographer writes,

> But the devil, who hates and envies what is good, could not endure to see such a resolution in a youth, but endeavoured to carry out against him what he had been wont to effect against others. First of all he tried to lead him away from the discipline, whispering to him the remembrance of his wealth, care for his sister, claims of kindred, love of money, love of glory, the various pleasures of the table and the other relaxations of life, and at last the difficulty of virtue and the labour of it; he suggested also the infirmity of the body and the length of the time. In a word he raised in his mind a great dust of debate, wishing to debar him from his settled purpose.[6]

A close reading of Antony's travails does not allow for a version Dante would admire, but rather one cloistered in the mind of the saint. The devil, long before he acquired capital letters and a name only given by a poor translation, was one who plagued the minds of the desert fathers. We see the saint clothed with deeds of righteousness struggling to ward off the devil. How did he finally do it? "But he, his mind filled with Christ and the nobility inspired by Him, and considering the spirituality of the soul, quenched the coal of the other's deceit."[7]

The mind is the devil's battlefield. However we may picture the devil—either as a being nearly equal in power to God, or as the darkness in each of us capable of so much evil we have to name it—to defeat our devil is still a part of the Christian mission (Luke 9:1). We are still called to liberate the world from its oppression. "To be

---

6. St. Athanasius of Alexandria, *Life of Antony*, (*NPNF* 4:196–7).
7. St. Athanasius of Alexandria, *Life of Antony*, (*NPNF* 4:197).

protected in this 'tabernacle from the contradiction of tongues,' is to be engulfed in the dark water. That soul, therefore, whose desires and affections are weaned, and whose faculties are in darkness, is set free from all the imperfections which war against the spirit, whether they proceed from the flesh, or from any other created thing. Such a soul may well say, 'In darkness and security.'"[8]

In both prayer and the Eucharist we find the power of liberation. Are they a magical elixir? No; instead, they are the manner in which we cleanse mind and spirit of the "contradiction of tongues." Prayer turns our mind to God. The Eucharist is equally a promise, a fulfillment, and a mission. Israel was promised a Messiah to bring about a new dispensation between God and his Creation. Jesus is the fulfillment. Now, we must take this symbol of Israel's story and the Gospel into the entire world. We do this with a mind armed with the power of prayer. "Thus there is need of much prayer and of discipline, that when a man has received through the Spirit the gift of discerning spirits, he may have power to recognize their characteristics: which of them are less and which more evil; of what nature is the special pursuit of each, and how each of them is overthrown and cast out. For their villainies and the changes in their plots are many... But we need not fear *the demons* suggestions—for by prayer, fasting, and faith in the Lord their attack immediately fails."[9] Both the prayer of the penitent and the giving of the Eucharist bind Satan.

The Second Prayer: Revelation 21:1–9

Our eyes long to see the new heaven and the new earth
Let the old give way to the new
Let the chaos of the sea find order
Our soul longs to see the holy city, New Jerusalem, descend
We are as a bride made ready for her husband

---

8. Saint John of the Cross, *The Dark Night of the Soul*, 425.
9. St. Athanasius of Alexandria, *Life of Antony*, (NPNF 4:202).

A Homily—The Eucharistic Vision

Behold! God is creating a new heaven and a new earth!
Bind us no longer to the things of old
Let us rejoice for the new creation!
Let the city be a place for happiness!
God will delight in us
There is no sorrow any longer![10]

O God, dwell with us
Make your tabernacle with your people
Walk again among us
O Lord, wipe our tears away,
Take all death away
Our God, remove from us the pain of this existence
Let the old things pass away.

Hear O Jerusalem, your husband has returned!
Spread out the feast
O God, you have removed the cloud of despair from us
The shadow of death is gone
You, O Lord, have wiped the tears from our eyes
You are our God and we will trust in you!
You have redeemed us!
Let us rejoice in your salvation![11]

Hear, O Heart, the words of the Lord
Behold, he makes all things new again
These are the words of God and they are faithful and true
Hear, O Soul, the words of God
It is finished. He is the Alpha and the Omega
He will gives to the thirsty the water of life freely
If we overcome, he will be our God; we will be his children

O Lord, you have responded to us in your time
This is your day of salvation and your covenant
We will be one people
You have freed the prisoners and given sight to the blind
We are your sheep and you have restored us

10. Isaiah 65:17–21.
11. Isaiah 25:6–10.

> We no longer hunger or thirst but are filled
> You lead us by your mercy, O Lord
> By the cool waters, our God leads us[12]
>
> O Lord, cleanse of our sins
> Let the second death no longer reign
> Take us from our cowardice and faithlessness
> Let us not be numbered among the murders and the wicked
> Show us your bride, the wife of the Lamb
>
> Listen, O Jerusalem, and understand
> Forget your people
> The king will desire your beauty
> Your king is our Lord; honor him
> All people will seek your grace with their works
> You are glorious as you descend
> You are righteous as you are presented to the king
> Let the people be led with joy
> Let us enter into the palace of the king[13]
>
> Amen

The End of Anxiety

The moment God became human is the moment the cosmos forever changed. An ancient hymn, forever enshrined in the Apostle Paul's epistle to the church at Philippi, reads,

> He was in the form of God
> yet he laid no claim to equality with God,
> but made himself nothing, assuming the form of a slave.
> Bearing the human likeness,
> sharing the human lot,
> he humbled himself, and was obedient,
> even to the point of death,
> death on a cross![14]

12. Isaiah 49:8–10.
13. Psalm 45:11–16.
14. Philippians 2:6–8.

A Homily—The Eucharistic Vision

Ancient Christian theologians argued about the quantity of this event. Did it happen more than once? Was it likely to happen again? Some held that it was such a momentous event it could only happen once, else the entirety of the miracle become degraded. While angels carried the words of God and are sometimes said to be God, because they represented God, the language of the incarnation is reserved only for the birth of Jesus Christ. This is the moment we celebrate from Advent until Christmas. We easily rest during this season in our expectation of the birth of Christ, perhaps because we know it has already happened. Yet, we are told Christ will return and we live anxiously for this. However, Christ has already returned and will always return. He returns in the taking of the Eucharist. Thus, Christ is truly with us when the sacrament is blessed and taken in the liturgy.

This is nearly meaningless when we are in such a state of grief caused by a myriad of reasons. We are told in this passage of Revelation about a moment God will wipe away all of tears. Yet, we still weep; we still mourn. We are promised many things in this passage those who believe Jesus has already physically return are struggling to account for.

We often forget we live in only one level of reality. Earth is not all there is. There are still the heavens, the ultimate reality. We are told in Hebrews 11.40, the saints who died under the Covenant of Moses reached perfection with the birth of the Church even though they lived and died under the promise. We cannot allow our momentary view, made with human eyes, to define reality for us. This is where prayer helps us. We begin seeking contemplative unity through prayer. We reach certain unity in the Eucharist. We will not reach the ultimate reality until we see the doors of life eternal. Everything given in Revelation is but a figure of heaven. We must understand this, or our lives will be led in fruitless anxiety.

The Third Prayer: Revelation 21:9–27

Rapture us, O Lord, to your great mountain
Show us the holy city, New Jerusalem, descending from heaven
From God New Jerusalem comes down
O God, you have given the city your glory
Her beauty is like precious stones

O Jerusalem, when you are built, you will be built forever
We will see all glorify and praise the king of heaven
From the gates of the city, sing hymns of joy
From the housetops, cry "Hallelujah!"
Shout, "Blessed is the God of Israel!"
His name will be blessed forever and ever[15]

Your walled city, O God, is too marvelous to behold
Twelve Angels stand at the Twelve Gates of the Twelve Tribes
Each wall is built upon the apostolic stones
These are the apostles to the Lamb

Let us arise for the light has come!
The glory of the Lord dawns upon us
Even when darkness covers the earth
Upon the Lord, the light will dawn
His glory will be seen
O Nations, you will walk by the radiance of our great king[16]

Let us measure the city, our great God!
The city is perfect, from Rome to Jerusalem it stands
The walls are jasper tone, the city gold but clear as glass
Every stone sought by humans adorn the foundation
At each gate is a pearl and each street is gold

We are no longer hated
Those who despised us bow at the feet of the Lord
We are the City of the Lord
We are the Zion of the Holy One of Israel

---

15. Tobit 13:16–17.
16. Isaiah 60:1–3.

God will make us his pride
He is our redeemer[17]

There is no more Temple
Our Lord God Almighty, our Lamb is the Temple
There is no sun or moon
It is the Glory of God illuminating the streets
The Lamb is its light
Come O Nations, and walk by the light of God.
O Kings of the Earth, bring your glory here!
There is no night; the gates are always open
O Nations, surrender here your honor and glory
There is no wickedness here, only the redeemed

Our God has promised to be our eternal light
His glory will cause the darkness to flee
Our days of mourning have come to and end
All of the people are righteous.
We will possess the city forever
Each of us will be a sign of the glory of God
O God, let your glory reign forever and ever[18]

Amen

The End of Darkness

After the commixture, the Orthodox Armenian Priest says,

> Holy Father, who hast called us by the name of Thine Only Begotten, and hast enlightened us through the baptism of the spiritual font, deign to accept this holy [sacrament] mystery for the forgiveness of our sins; stamp upon us the graces of the Holy Ghost, as Thou didst on the holy apostles who tasted of it, and became the cleansers of the whole world. And now, Lord and beneficent Father, make this communion a part of the evening meal of the

---

17. Isaiah 60:14–16.
18. Isaiah 60:19–22.

> Apostles, by removing the darkness of our sins. Look not upon the unworthiness of my sins; neither withhold from me the grace of Thy Holy Spirit. But according to Thine unspeakable charity, grant that this [sacrament] be for the expiation of sins, and for the loosing of trespasses. As our Lord Jesus Christ did promise and say, "Whosoever eats My Flesh and drinks My Blood shall live for ever;" therefore, now make it to be to us for the expiation of sins, so that those who shall eat and drink of it, may bless and glorify the father, and the son, and the holy Ghost, now and ever, world without end. Amen.[19]

The Temple was destroyed in 70, forcing Jews to seek other means of fulfilling the sacrificial demands of the Law. Without the Temple, what would they do? Paul writes the Law teaches us of our sins (Romans 7–8). We cannot read Paul without understanding how intimately the Law and Temple were connected. Even those who followed Jesus struggled to understand this new world. The Jews who did not believe in Messiah Jesus migrated to Rabbinical Judaism, enshrining the Temple in later literary traditions. Jews who believed in Jesus Christ met this new reality in a similar, but different way.

In Revelation, we are met with the reality of a Temple-absent religion. This was very much true and still remains a painful physical reality for Jews. John, speaking to the needs of his community, shows them the new Temple. It is not one made with hands (Mark 14:58; Acts 7:48), but one centered on the Risen Christ, present only in the sacrifice of the Eucharist. Suddenly, we need no Temple *except* the one that is our God and the Lamb (Revelation 21:22). This Temple is light and so much light we need no sun or moon. It attracts not just one people, but also all peoples, even those peoples who previously rebelled against God (Revelation 21:24). This light cleanses us every whit because it is the Son (1 John 1:5–7). Jesus himself is the light of the Temple, the Church, and the World; there is no limit to where Jesus shines. Darkness is gone.

---

19. Hammond, *Liturgies: Eastern and Western*, 163.

The rhetorical device at the end of this chapter is confusing, but it has a hidden meaning. Nothing unclean will enter. No one not written in the Lamb's Book of Life shall find a place there.

A Prayer of Adoration

O Great God, you have bound the dragon
In the abyss the devil is chained
By your sacrifice we are saved

Judge us, O Holy God
Let the Prophets and the Apostles examine us
Give life to the dead
Bless those in the first resurrection
Protect us waiting the second

O God, your throne is marvelous
All stand before, even the greatest and the lowliest
All are judged by their deeds
In the end, only death and the grave are thrown away

O God and the Lamb
Tabernacle with us
Shine up us with your light
Send away the darkness of our sins
Your bride is ready.

Make all things new, O Lord!
You are the Alpha and the Omega
You are the beginning and the end of all things
Give us your Holy Spirit

19

The Prayer of Dismissal

> Keep us in peace, O Christ our God, under the protection of Thy holy
> and venerable Cross ... and make us meet with thanksgivings
> to glorify Thee with the Father and with the Holy Ghost;
> now and ever, world without end. Amen.[1]

The contemplation draws to a close. The service is done; our time in prayer is nearing the finish. We sense the quietness departing us as our voice turns to a whisper, while the world awaits us with a chaotic crescendo of clamor. We are drawn outside from our momentary monastic cell to a world where captivity is called freedom, darkness named light and individualism labeled society. There needs not be much thought to our closing words, only to focus our mind steadily on Christ.

The First Prayer: Revelation 22:1–9

O Lord, bring us to the river of the water of Life
It comes from the throne of God and the Lamb
It flows in the middle of heaven

---

1. This is the final benediction in the Armenian Church. Hammond, *Liturgies: Eastern and Western*, 168.

The Prayer of Dismissal

Our God, let us eat from the tree of life
It bears twelve fruits, one each month
From its leaves come the healing for the nations

Our souls rest only in God
From the Lord comes our salvation
He alone is my rock and my salvation
Our enemies war not against us, but against God
Their delights are lies and sins
Our souls rest only in God[2]

O Lord, we long for end to Adam's curse
We seek the throne of God and the Lamb
We desire nothing but to be the slaves of God
Let us see your face
Mark us with your name
On that day, in that place, there will be no more night
In that city there is no sun
You, O Great God, our Lord, you are the light
Your light will shine forever and ever

Let our souls find rest in God
From him alone comes our hope
The Lord alone is our fortress and we will not fall
He is our deliver, our rock, our refuge
We will trust in God always
Our hearts belong to the Lord![3]

Your words are truly faithful, Our Lord, Our God
You have shown us what is happening
You will come quickly so let us listen to John's words
He was the first who heard these things
When he did, he fell down to worship
O God, let us heed the words of that angel
Let us only worship you, Our King.

Are not but a vapor?
Is our strength nothing more than an illusion?

2. Psalm 62:1–5.
3. Psalm 62:6–9.

> Even standing together, we are nothing
> Let us not trust in others for salvation
> All hope placed there is empty!
> Let us not set our heart on wealth
> Only God has strength
> Only the Lord has mercy![4]
>
> Amen

The Never-Ending Rapture

The second verse of this chapter tells of a tree of life, like Eden's. It is no longer forbidden, but now holds therapeutic elixir meant to bring about holiness and healing to all nations. Note the nations and their kings in this conclusion. They are the very ones who have so labored in vain to plot a rebellion against God and the ones cast into punishment. Yet, they are here with us now, partaking of the Tree of Life. They show God's powerful forgiveness. Indeed, all things are restored. This is a panoramic view of Creation, providing a heavenly view of the whole of the covenant's history.[5] This is not just a chapter about endings, but about new beginnings.

Perhaps it is something of a cliché; however, in many of our bibles, the words THE END appear in the white space below Revelation 22:21. This is our very modern way of thinking of things. We know there is no end to the Kingdom of God. This is affirmed in the Nicene Creed of 381 by the phrase, "*whose kingdom shall have no end.*" If Revelation 22:21 were really the end, we would not have the Great Tradition to guide the Church. If this were really the end, we would but take the Eucharist once and hope it had cured us of our malicious malady.

What we must understand is just as with each Saturday giving way to a Sunday and Sunday to a Monday and so on, Revelation does not simply end here. The Christian life does not simply end here in

---

4. Psalm 62:10–12.
5. Frye, *The Great Code*, 137.

God's cosmic theatre. It does not find an end in the liturgical drama where the Gospel is acted out and spoken weekly. Instead, all of our Christian participation is simply the beginning. Revelation and Genesis are connected by the tree of life, presenting us a theological circle.

Paul Tillich writes, "The theologian as theologian is committed to a concrete expression of the ultimate concern, religiously speaking, of a special revelatory experience. On the basis of this concrete experience he makes his universal claims, as Christianity did in terms of the statement that Jesus Christ is the Logos. This circle can be described as an ellipse (not a geometrical circle) and described in terms of two central points—the existential question and the theological answer."[6] We see this in a complete, heavenly view of the Christian canon. The existential question asked in Genesis is given a theological answer in the praxis of Christianity, neatly encapsulated in the final book. The high/low points of the ellipse are always Christ, but we must note the ellipse, just an oddly shaped circle, never ends. It continues.

The Second Prayer: Revelation 22:10–21

O my Jesus, do not withhold your words from us
Your time is always near
Let those who are wrong still do wrong
Let those who are in sin still sin
But let the righteous and the holy keep holy
Come quickly, Lord Jesus, and bring your reward
Give to each of us according to our works
You are the Alpha and the Omega
In every end, your bring a beginning

Let us give our praise to God!
Praise God's holy name! He is the Most High!
We will proclaim God's love from the morning to the evening

---

6. Tillich, *Systematic Theology, Vol. II*, 14–5.

Praying in God's Theater

> O God, you give us joy by the works of your hands!
> How magnificent are your works, O God!
> How deep are your mysteries![7]

We will wash our robes in the blood of the Lamb
Let us enter the gates of the city and eat of the tree of life
Let the sinners remained outside the gates
You, Jesus, are our witness
You are both the son and the king of David
You are our bright morning star

> How magnificent are your works, O God!
> How deep are your mysteries!
> The senseless person does not know you
> While sinners thrive, their destiny awaits them
> You, O Lord, reign forever!
> Let your enemies scatter![8]

We pray to hear the Spirit and the Bride bid us come
We will answer, Come!
The thirsty will answer, Come!
The water of life is freely given!
Lord, we treasure the words of your prophets
Let us add nothing to it, nor take away.
Take nothing you have given away from us
Come quickly, Lord Jesus, Come.
Amen.

> Our God has given us his strength
> Our enemies will be defeated
> The righteous shall prosper in the house of the Lord
> They shall grow in the courts of our God!
> Let us proclaim the righteousness of the Lord![9]

Amen

---

7. Psalm 92:1–6.
8. Psalm 92:6–10.
9. Psalm 92:11–16.

The Prayer of Dismissal

Come!

> O Lord, who blessest them that bless Thee, and makest them holy that put their trust in Thee, save alive Thy congregation, and bless Thine inheritance; maintain the fulness of Thy Church, and sanctify those who in love come to greet the majesty of Thy House. Glorify us with Thy divine power, and forsake not those who put their trust in Thee. Grant peace to the whole world, to the Churches, priests, Christian kings, to their armies, and to the whole of this congregation. For all good gifts and all perfect gifts come down from thee above, who art the Father of light; and unto Thee belong glory, dominion, and honour, now and ever, world without end. Amen.[10]

Our time in prayer is at a close. We have contemplated the mysteries of the divine and come to realize we know nothing more about God than we did before. Have we considered an earnest prayer for our enemies? Not simply one devoted to their rightward track, but one where we intercede for them when they get off course? Where we take their due portion of the wrath of God? In doing so, may we hope to burn the beam out of our eye? There is no harm in becoming more Christ-like in this regard, to follow his example of absorbing the violent wrath due the sinner.

Likewise, have we considered the medicine afforded by the Eucharist? What wondrous salve it is to our souls. Regardless of our theological understanding of it, it is so ordered by God. Thus, if even in obedience taken, it becomes to us a deed remembered. As St. Thomas Aquinas writes, "Thou art the Bread of Heaven, my Jesus, and I find Thee at this Table of God. Thou art the medicine of the soul, and I find Thee the true Manna in the Holy Eucharist. Enlighten me, my Jesus, and purify me, and save me from the second death."[11]

---

10. Hammond, ed., *Liturgies: Eastern and Western*, 167.
11. Aquinas, *The Bread of Life*, 230.

When we kneel in prayer, we do so in contemplative our unity with God. Does this not then put us in the mind of grief? We are sinners, wretched. Yes, we are redeemed and filled with grace, but we stumble. We are still in darkness, being brought to the light. It is a process—we *are* saved, we *are being* saved, and we *will be* saved. It is not a momentary salvation commitment, but a continued flood of God's gift. When we begin to contemplate our life with God, do we not see how utterly deprived we are of any self-reliance? Our independence is a myth, a façade. We pretend we may find our own path, but in our deepest moments, when we are able to find that thin place where God communicates with us and we to God, we realize how void our life is of self-control. Then, we come to realize just how important it is this unity with God.

We are placed in union with God in baptism, but we grow to the "unity inherent in our faith and in our knowledge of the Son of God."[12] Scripture speaks of this constant path to God, with the divine standing at the far corner beckoning us with a simple word, "Come."

> First of all, the bride of Christ who wishes to rise to the summit of perfect life should start at the level of her own self. Forgetting the material world, she must enter the hidden recesses of her conscience, there to explore, examine, and weigh with attentive care all her faults, habits, affections, and deeds; all her sins, both past and present. Whatever fault she finds within herself, let her repent it with sincere grief.[13]

Conclusion

Our journey to the open door is not one of an immediate step, but one of constant *ora et labora*. We pray and work. At the beginning of Revelation, we are enjoined to meet God through Christ. This is the beginning, but as John has showed us, we are not left only with an

---

12. Ephesians 4:13.
13. Saint Bonaventure, "Mystical Opuscula," 212.

image of God; the image is but the beginning. We move from there, following ancient rabbis into seven levels of prayers. We have our vision of God, one long vision from our resting place in the thin places between heaven and earth. We watch as the diadems are thrown, angels sing, and the prayers travel to God in the incense.

We watch as a heavenly liturgy comes into full view. We are on the stage of God's theatre. Just as in the Gospel, Jesus takes center stage and his cross the ultimate curtain fall, God is shown before us in complete control, with all other performers as backdrops.

Our thematic prayer follows the course of ancient liturgies, reaching out to us and back towards Revelation. We cannot shake loose the Great Tradition of Christianity, but find ourselves mourning over its neglect. How often might we find food nestled in the crevices of history's theologians? Perhaps, we wonder, do the ancients know more about the spiritual life of the Christian than we moderns?

The Table—Christ—is prepared and we are beckoned to it. We contemplate whether or not we are able to partake and we are given time to make sure we may justly receive it. We pray for our enemies, believing God could lose no one, even in his anger at their rebellion. After all, we pray, we were the worse of sinners ourselves! If God can spare us, might he so too spare those who are needed to show his grace? We humbly pray the hope of ancient and not-so-ancient theologians will be found sure. We pray for a place where sin is purged, if not in this life, then in the next.

We then, in our mind, meet the Table. We contemplate the Eucharist and we discover it anew with the ancients and ourselves as the certain unity between God and us. We then hear of the benefits of this unity. Because we were unable to make the journey ourselves, God has come to us. Where we are weak, he gives us strength. There is no more darkness. We are cleansed in every way. Then, we are pulled away from this thin place, snatched back into a dreadful reality. It is not the ultimate reality, but one we create through rebellion and selfish perception. We will travel onward, until the next time we are able to gather again, either in prayer or to take the Eucharist.

"We know that when any one of us falls, he falls alone; but no one is saved alone. He who is saved is saved in the Church, as a member of her, and in unity with all her other members. If anyone believes, he is in the community of faith; if anyone loves, he is in the communion of love; if anyone prays, he is in the communion of prayer."[14]

A Prayer of Adoration

O Great God, prepare us for your world
Let us drink from the river of life
Give us your Holy Spirit
Let us be healed to heal
Let us be your light to the world

O God the Son, give us your word
Come soon; give us strength
Your time stands now
The world is ready for the Gospel.

O Holy Spirit, say to the bride,
Come
Same to those who hear your words
Come
Give us your water to drink

Come soon, Lord Jesus
Heal our land
Give us your body and blood
Be the medicine to our souls.

---

14. A. S. Khomiakov, *The Church Is One* (rev. translated William Palmer, with an introduction essay by N. Zernov; London: Fellowship of St Alban and St. Sergius, 1968), 38.

Afterword

Major Jeff Carter, Salvation Army

> "Speech is the organ of this present world.
> Silence is a mystery of the world to come."
>
> ST. ISAAC THE SYRIAN[1]

What can I say after Joel? I come from a non-liturgical, non-sacramental denomination (The Salvation Army). I can offer no elaboration on the beauty of the liturgy, and though I appreciate the sacraments (especially the Eucharist /communion) it is not a part of my normal worship practice. And I have always—always—struggled with prayer. I pray, but often wonder if I'm being heard. So what can I say? I would rather be silent. But Joel asked me to write, and I said that I would.

> There is no life without prayer. Without prayer
> there is only madness and horror.
>
> VASILII ROZANOV[2]

---

1. Quoted in Ware, *The Orthodox Way*, 178.
2. Quoted in Ware, *The Orthodox Way*, 105.

For most of my life I have heard stories of how "God answers prayer,"—like the story about George Muller who needed food to feed the children in his orphanage, but had none. He prayed and there was a knock at the door. A baker was standing there with an armload of bread. Moments later came the milkman with ten large cans of milk for the children. George Muller prayed about everything, and recorded his prayers (and their answers) in his journals—30,000 of them answered by God![3]

Me? I don't know if I could tell you of one definitively answered prayer—not, at least of the George Muller variety. I've seen no miraculous healings. I've never had someone knock on my door to deliver the precise thing I needed at the very moment I needed it. When my wife and I were losing our first child in an early miscarriage, I prayed—desperately, fervently—but the child was still lost.

And yet, I continue to pray. I continue to confront the world by approaching God with my spiritual, emotional, and physical burdens. Because if I give up prayer, then only madness and horror remain, and I refuse to allow those forces to roll over me.

John's Revelation is a drama of prayer and of worship and of battle. We pray through the Revelation then as an expression of heartfelt worship for the God who has created and redeemed us. We also pray the Revelation in order to be readied for the war. To be strengthened. To be empowered. To have our hope and courage restored.

We pray in the face of injustice and oppression. We pray against the exploitation of women and children and we pray for the exploited ones. We pray that the addicts might be released from the chains of their desires. We pray that the hungry may be fed, that the sick may be made well. We pray that the fallen might be lifted up and that the broken may be mended.

We pray that wars may be ended, that conflicts may cease, that our weapons of destruction may be melted down and transformed into instruments of provision and succor.

---

3. At least that's how the story was told to me — repeatedly.

We pray for justice to roll down like a mighty river. We pray that sin might be renounced and repented, replaced by the holiness that comes from the sacred spirit of God.

And in all these things we are praying that the glorious image of God may be restored to the bruised and broken reeds of humanity. In all these things we are praying to see the victory won by that Lamb who was slain. In all these prayers we are praying for the incarnation—the embodiment of that victory in the world around us.

> "...we should work as if everything depended upon our efforts, and pray as if everything depended upon God."[4]
>
> ST. AUGUSTINE

And so we pray.

---

4. *Catechism of the Catholic Church*, in paragraphs 2302–317.

Bibliography

à Kempis, Thomas. *The Imitation of Christ*. Oak Harbor, WA: Logos Research Systems, 1996.
Aquinas, Thomas. *The Bread of Life, or, St. Thomas Aquinas on the Adorable Sacrament of the Altar*. London: Burns and Oates, 1879.
———. *Summa Theologica*. Translated by the Fathers of the English Dominican Province. Bellingham, WA: Logos Bible Software, 2009.
Aretaeus. *The Extant Works of Aretaeus, The Cappadocian*. Translated by Francis Adams. Kansas City, Missouri: Milford House Inc., 2005.
Armstrong, Dave. *Biblical Catholic Answers for John Calvin*. Dave Armstrong, 2010
Balzer, Tracy. *Thin Places: An Evangelical Journey into Celtic Christianity*. Abilene, Tex.: Leafwood, 2007.
Barber, Michael. *Coming Soon: Unlocking the Book of Revelation and Applying Its Lessons Today*. Steubenville, OH: Emmaus Road Publishing, 2005.
Baxter, Richard and William Orme. *The Practical Works of the Rev. Richard Baxter: Volume XII*. London: James Duncan, 1830.
Benedict XVI. *Caritas in Veritate*. Vatican City: Libreria Editrice Vaticana, 2009.
Bernard. *St. Bernard's Sermons on the Canticle of Canticles, Volume 2*. Translated by A Priest of Mount Melleray. Dublin: Browne and Nolan, 1920.
Bonaventure. "Breviloquium." *The Works of Bonaventure: Cardinal Seraphic Doctor and Saint, Vol 2*. Translated by José De Vinck. Paterson, NJ: St. Anthony Guild Press, 1963.
———. "Mystical Opuscula." *The Works of Bonaventure: Cardinal Seraphic Doctor and Saint* Translated by José De Vinck. Paterson, NJ: St. Anthony Guild Press, 1960.
Boxall, Ian. *The Revelation of Saint John*. Black's New Testament Commentary. London: Continuum, 2006.
Brightman, F. E. *Liturgies: Eastern and Western*. Oxford: Clarendon Press, 1896. Edited by Thomas Harding. Cambridge: Cambridge University Press, 1849.
Butler, Alban. *The Lives of the Fathers, Martyrs and Other Principal Saints, Vol. IV*. New York: P. J. Kenedy, 1903.
Chapman, Mark D. *The Coming Crisis: The Impact of Eschatology on Theology in Edwardian England*. Journal for the Study of the New Testament Supplement Series. Sheffield: Sheffield Academic Press, 2001.
Chazon, Esther G., et al. *Liturgical Perspectives: Prayer and Poetry in Light of the Dead Sea Scrolls*. Leiden; Boston: Brill, 2003.
Chesterton, G. K. *All Things Considered*. New York: John Lane Company, 1909.
Chilton, David. *The Days of Vengeance: An Exposition of the Book of Revelation*. Ft. Worth, Tex.: Dominion Press, 1987.

Bibliography

Chrysostom, St. John and St. Basil the Great. *The Divine Liturgies Of Our Fathers Among The Saints John Chrysostom And Basil The Great With That Of The Presanctified: Preceded By The Hesperinos And The Orthros.* Translated by James Nathaniel William Beauchamp Robertson. 1894. LaVergne, TN: Kessinger Publishing, 2010.

Cross, F. L. and Elizabeth A. Livingstone. *The Oxford Dictionary of the Christian Church.* Oxford: Oxford University Press, 2005.

Denzinger, Henry, et al. *The Sources of Catholic Dogma.* St. Louis, MO: B. Herder Book Co., 1954.

Drane, Augusta Theodosia. *The History of St. Catherine of Siena and Her Companions: With a Translation of Her Treatise on Consummate Perfection, Vol. 2, Third Edition.* London: Longmans, Green & Co., 1899.

Edwards, Jonathan. *The Works of Jonathan Edwards, Vol. 2.* Bellingham, WA: Logos Bible Software, 2008.

Evans, G. R. and J. Robert Wright. *The Anglican Tradition: a Handbook of Sources.* London: SPCK, 1991.

Frye, Northrop. *The Great Code: The Bible and Literature.* London: Harcourt, 1981.

García Martínez, Florentino and Eibert J. C. Tigchelaar. *The Dead Sea Scrolls Study Edition.* Leiden: Brill, 1998.

Hahn, Scott W. *Kinship by Covenant: a Canonical Approach to the Fulfillment of God's Saving Promises.* New Haven: Yale University Press, 2009.

Hammond, C. E. *Liturgies: Eastern and Western.* Oxford: Clarendon Press, 1878.

Hefele, Charles Joseph. *A History of the Councils of the Church, Volume 4.* Translated by William R. Clark. Edinburgh: T&T Clark, 1895.

Hemer, Colin J. *The Letters to the Seven Churches of Asia in Their Local Setting.* Grand Rapids, MI: William B. Eerdmans Publishing Company, 2001.

Henry, Carl F. H. *God, Revelation, and Authority.* Wheaton, IL: Crossway Books, 1999.

John Paul II. *Redemptoris Missio.* Vatican City: Libreria Editrice Vaticana, 1990.

Johnson, Lawrence J. *Worship in the Early Church: An Anthology of Historical Sources, Vol. 2.* Collegeville, MN: Liturgical Press, 2009.

Keener, Craig S. *The IVP Bible Background Commentary: New Testament.* Downers Grove, IL: InterVarsity Press, 1993.

Kierkegaard, Søren. *Purity of Heart is To Will One Thing.* Translated by Douglas Steere. New York: Harper and Brothers, 1948.

Koenig, John. *The Feast of the World's Redemption: Eucharistic Origins and Christian Mission.* Harrisburg, Pa.: Trinity Press International, 2000.

Lépicier, Cardinal Alexis Henri Marie. *Indulgences, Their Origin, Nature, and Development (1895).* Cornell University Library, 2009.

Lewis, C. S. *Letters to Malcolm Chiefly on Prayer: Reflections on the Intimate Dialogue Between Man and God.* San Diego: Harcourt, Inc., 1992.

Macomber, W.F. "The Oldest Known Text of the Anaphora of the Apostles Addai and Mari." OPC 32 (1966) 335-71.

McKenzie, J. L. *The Jewish World in New Testament Times, A Catholic Commentary on Holy Scripture* Edited by Bernard Orchard and Edmund F. Sutcliffe. Toronto: Thomas Nelson, 1953.

Migne, Jean-Paul, ed. *Patrologiae Latinae Cursus Completus Omnium.* SS. Patrum, Doctorum Scriptorum Ecclesiasticorum. 217 vols. Turnholti: Typographi Brepols Editores Pontificii, 1844–1855.

Mowry, Lucetta. "Revelation 4-5 and Early Christian Liturgical Usage," *Journal of Biblical Literature*, Vol. 71, No. 2 (1952), 75-84.

Murray, Robert. *Symbols of Church and Kingdom: A Study in Early Syriac Tradition*. London: T&T Clark, 1975.

Newman, John Henry. *An Essay on the Development of Christian Doctrine*. London: James Toovey, 1845.

O'Brien, John. *A History of the Mass and Its Ceremonies in the Eastern and Western Church*. New York: The Catholic Publication Society Co., 1881.

Oden, Thomas C. *The Word of Life: Systematic Theology, Vol. II*. San Francisco: Harper San Francisco, 1992.

Oecumenius. "Oecumenius, Commentary on the Apocalypse." In *Greek Commentaries on Revelation*. Ancient Christian Texts. Translated by William C. Weinrich. Downers Grove, Ill.: IVP Academic, 2011.

Origen. *Treatise on the Passover and Dialogue with Heraclides*. Translated by Robert J. Daly. Ancient Christian Writers, 54. New York: Paulist Press, 1992.

Perrin, Nicholas. *Jesus the Temple*. Grand Rapids, MI: Society for Promoting Christian Knowledge, 2010.

Ratzinger, Joseph. *The Spirit of the Liturgy*. Translated by John Saward. San Francisco: Ignatius Press, 2000.

Rausch, Thomas P. *Catholicism in the Third Millennium*. Collegeville, Minn.: Liturgical Press, 2003.

Ritzema, Elliot. *300 Quotations for Preachers from the Reformation*. Bellingham, WA: Logos Bible Software, 2013.

Ritzema, Elliot and Elizabeth Vince. *300 Quotations for Preachers from the Puritans*. Bellingham, WA: Logos Bible Software, 2013.

Roberts, Alexander, et al. *The Ante-Nicene Father, Volume I: The Apostolic Fathers with Justin Martyr and Irenaeus*. Buffalo, NY: Christian Literature Company, 1885.

———. *The Ante-Nicene Fathers, Volume II: Fathers of the Second Century: Hermas, Tatian, Athenagoras, Theophilus, and Clement of Alexandria*. Buffalo, NY: Christian Literature Company, 1885.

———. *The Ante-Nicene Fathers, Volume VI: Fathers of the Third Century: Gregory Thaumaturgus, Dionysius the Great, Julius Africanus, Anatolius and Minor Writers, Methodius, Arnobius*. Buffalo, NY: Christian Literature Company, 1886.

———. *The Ante-Nicene Fathers, Volume V: Fathers of the Third Century: Hippolytus, Cyprian, Novatian, Appendix*. Buffalo, NY: Christian Literature Company, 1886.

———. *The Ante-Nicene Fathers, Volume VII: Fathers of the Third and Fourth Centuries: Lactantius, Venantius, Asterius, Victorinus, Dionysius, Apostolic Teaching and Constitutions, Homily, and Liturgies*. Buffalo, NY: Christian Literature Company, 1886.

Ignatius of Loyola. *The Spiritual Exercises of St. Ignatius of Loyola*. Translated by Elder Mullan. New York: P. J. Kenedy & Sons, 1914.

John of the Cross. *The Ascent of Mount Carmel*. Translated by Benedict Zimmermann, and David Lewis. London: Thomas Baker, 1906.

———. *The Dark Night of the Soul*. Translated by David Lewis, and Nicholas Patrick Wiseman. London: Longman, Green, Longman, Roberts, & Green, 1864.

Schaff, Philip and Henry Wace. *A Select Library of the Nicene and Post-Nicene Fathers of the Christian Church, Second Series: St. Athanasius: Select Works and Letters Vol. 4*. New York: Christian Literature Company, 1892.

Bibliography

———. *A Select Library of the Nicene and Post-Nicene Fathers of the Christian Church, Second Series: S. Cyril of Jerusalem, S. Gregory Nazianzen Vol. 7*. New York: Christian Literature Company, 1894.

Schiffman, Lawrence H. *Reclaiming the Dead Sea Scrolls: The History of Judaism, The Background of Christianity, The Lost Library of Qumran*. New York: Double Day Publishing Group, 1994.

Schmidt, Francis. *How the Temple Thinks: Identity and Social Cohesion in Ancient Judaism*. Sheffield, England: Sheffield Academic Press, 2001.

Simkins, William Washington. *The Oriental and Grecian Philosophy. Nature's Good and Evil: The Fourth Nationality with Its Four Grand Empires. The Fall of the Political and Ecclesiastical World. The Church in its Different Places and Conditions. The Kingdom of God*. University of Michigan Library, 1879. Reprint

Snyder, Howard A. *Yes in Christ: Wesleyan Reflections on Gospel, Mission and Culture*. Toronto: Clements Academic, 2010.

Stakemeier, E. *De Mariologia et Oecumenismo*. K. Balic, ed., Rome: Academia, 1962.

Stone, Darwell. *The Eucharistic Sacrifice*. Eugene, OR: Wipf & Stock, 2006.

———. *A History of the Doctrine of the Holy Eucharist*. Eugene, OR: Wipf & Stock, 2006.

Streett, R. Alan. *Subversive Meals: An Analysis of the Lord's Supper Under Roman Domination During the First Century*. Eugene, OR.: Pickwick Publications, 2013.

Taylor, G.W. *John Wesley and the Anglo-Catholic Revival*. London: SPCK, 1905. No pages. Online: http://anglicanhistory.org/misc/taylor_wesley.html.

Trafton, Joseph L. *Reading Revelation: a Literary and Theological Commentary*. Reading the New Testament Series. Macon, GA: Smyth & Helwys Publishing, 2005.

Turner, Paul. *At the Supper of the Lamb: A Pastoral and Theological Commentary on the Mass*. Chicago, IL: Liturgy Training Publications), 2011.

von Balthasar, Hans Urs. *The Glory of the Lord: A Theological Aesthetics I: Seeing the Form* (trans. Erasmo Leiva-Merikakis; San Francisco: Ignatius Press, 2009.

Weinrich, William C., et al. *Revelation*. Ancient Christian Commentary on Scripture. Downers Grove, IL: InterVarsity Press, 2005.

Weiss, Johannes. *Christ, The Beginnings of Dogma*. Translated by V.D. Davis. Boston: American Unitarian Association, 1911.

Wesley, John. *Explanatory Notes Upon the New Testament*. Fourth American Edition.; New York: J. Soule and T. Mason, 1818.

———. *Sermons, on Several Occasions*. Oak Harbor, WA: Logos Research Systems, Inc., 1999.

West, Jim. *'Christ Our Captain': An Introduction to Huldrych Zwingli*. Quartz Hill, CA: Quartz Hill Publishing House, 2011.

Wiersbe, Warren W. *The Bible Exposition Commentary*. Wheaton, IL: Victor Books, 1996.

www.ingramcontent.com/pod-product-compliance
Lightning Source LLC
Chambersburg PA
CBHW060602230426
43670CB00011B/1926